Focus

Prentice Hall LIFE

If life is what you make it, then making it better starts here.

What we learn today can change our lives tomorrow. It can change our goals or change our minds; open up new opportunities or simply inspire us to make a difference. That's why we have created a new breed of books that do more to help you make more of *your* life.

Whether you want more confidence or less stress, a new skill or a different perspective, we've designed *Prentice Hall Life* books to help you to make a change for the better. Together with our authors we share a commitment to bring you the brightest ideas and best ways to manage your life, work and wealth.

In these pages we hope you'll find the ideas you need for the life *you* want. Go on, help yourself.

It's what you make it

* * *

FOCUS

The power of targeted thinking

Jurgen Wolff

Harlow, England • London • New York • Boston • San Francisco • Toronto • Sydney • Singapore • Hong Kong
Tokyo • Seoul • Taipei • New Delhi • Cape Town • Madrid • Mexico City • Amsterdam • Munich • Paris • Milan

PEARSON EDUCATION LIMITED

Edinburgh Gate
Harlow CM20 2JE
Tel: +44(0)1279 623623
Fax: +44(0)1279 431059
Website: www.pearsoned.co.uk

First published in Great Britain in 2008

ISBN: 978-0-273-71544-3

British Library Cataloguing-in-Publication Data
A catalogue record for this book is available from the British Library

Library of Congress Cataloging-in-Publication Data
Wolff, Jurgen M. (Jurgen Michael), 1948–
   Focus : the power of targeted thinking / Jurgen
Wolff.
        p. cm.
   Includes bibliographical references and index.
   ISBN 978-0-273-71544-3 (alk. paper)
  1. Attention. I. Title.
   BF321.W65 2008
   153.7´33--dc22

2008006175

10 9 8 7 6 5 4 3 2
11 10 09 08

Typeset in 10pt Iowan by 3
Printed and bound in Great Britain by Henry Ling Limited, at the Dorset Press, Dorchester, DT1 1HD

The publisher's policy is to use paper manufactured from sustainable forests.

Contents

Part 4 Putting it all together 181

Foreword

By Bob Cochran, co-creator and executive producer of *24*

If there was ever a man in need of focused and efficient time management techniques, Jack Bauer is that man. Every year, like clockwork (pun intended), he faces a day in which he has twenty-four hours to save the world. He's managed to do it six times as of this writing, but it gets a bit harder every year. At least that's what he tells me.

As a television writer and producer, I don't have to save the world (luckily for the world) but, like everyone else, I do have a limited amount of time each day to accomplish whatever must be done in order to achieve my longer term goals. And, as Jurgen Wolff suggests, focus is the key.

On any given day of a television show, while one episode is being filmed, a second is being edited, a third scored, a fourth storied, a fifth rewritten, a sixth prepped and cast ... well, you get the idea. Deciding where and how to direct your energy, hour by hour, day by day, is the surest, and in fact the only, road to success. This book will help you find that road and, more importantly, stay on it.

The book is loaded with insights and fresh approaches to the problem of managing time. A few of my favourites include applying the 80/20 rule to your own life (instead of to a corporation); how to recognize harmful behaviour patterns that you may be hiding from yourself; and how to leverage your already-existing strengths to help you succeed in a broader range of activities. I could go on, but just glance through the pages and you'll probably come up with a few favourites of your own very quickly.

In short, *Focus: The power of targeted thinking* lives up to its title. I have a copy in my office, and the next time I see Jack Bauer I think I'll give him a copy, too. I just hope he has time to read it.

Introduction

How creating focus will change your life

Have you ever felt frustrated by knowing that you could do a lot better in your career and the other parts of your life, but you just can't seem to do it? Have you ever been angry with yourself because you're not achieving your potential and time is slipping by? Do you have a vision of the life you'd like, but no clear path for how to get there?

If those statements ring a bell, you've come to the right place. This book isn't about *what*, it's about *how*. You probably already know what you want from life (and if you don't, Chapter 1 will help you clarify it). Probably the big question in your mind is, "How do I get there from here?"

What this change requires is focus but, frankly, the world conspires to prevent you from having that kind of focus. It's not surprising that you feel scattered and distracted. You are being bombarded every waking minute with advertising messages that pull you in one direction, the expectations of family members and colleagues that pull you in another, haunted by the ghost of goals you may have set for yourself but didn't reach for reasons that weren't your fault. On top of that you're expected to be reachable 24/7, so any little scraps of time that you might have had for reflection are snatched away from you. Under these circumstances, it would be amazing if you were able to focus.

Well, prepare to be amazed – and amazing.

This book will take you, step by step, through the process of deciding what you really want, figuring out what has stopped you in the past, becoming aware of the disruptive influences in the way you use time (and how to fix them), and learning how to overcome the factors that hold back the vast majority of people. Finally, it will show you how to put all this information together into a plan you can follow again and again as you set new goals for yourself. The methods revealed in this book will become automatic habits that lead to success with less and less effort on your part.

Many of the techniques in this book are new. They are based on the fact that the old methods just don't work anymore, especially for right-brain people. The traditional time management techniques were developed during the simpler industrial age to make people doing repetitive tasks more efficient. Using them in today's atmosphere of 24/7 connectivity and constant demands leads to frantic multitasking and firefighting. The result: lots of activity, not much achievement.

If you have tried the traditional methods of time management and found them time-consuming, restrictive, and ineffective, the odds are you are a right-brain person. If you like variety, have good intuition, and enjoy new challenges but hate being trapped in old routines, this book has been written especially for you.

Today the need is for creativity, flexibility, and making smart choices. FOCUS shows you how to identify what's most important and how to direct all your energy, without distractions, to the tasks that propel you toward success.

I know the techniques you are about to learn work because they've worked for me and for hundreds of people who have participated in my *Create Your Future* workshops. I predict that you're going to enjoy using breakthrough techniques like the Alter Ego strategy for getting any task done in record time, and the MAD strategy for turbo-charging any project that is moving too slowly or in which you feel stuck. Here's a quick roadmap of what you're going to experience:

Maybe you've heard of the 80/20 principle before, but odds are you've not been shown how actually to apply it to your work and personal life. By focusing on the 20% of your life that gives you the greatest value, you increase your success exponentially – that's what you'll learn to do in Chapter 1.

In Chapter 2, you'll translate that into a big, inspiring goal, but not until you've found out the one trap that dooms most goals to failure, and how to avoid it.

In Chapter 3 you'll learn how time patterns work and figure out how your time patterns have distracted you from the success of which you are capable. You'll also discover how to put more effective patterns to use.

Have you noticed how easy it is to know what to do next, but how hard it is to actually do it? Chapter 4 reveals the hidden obstacle that stops most people from reaching their goals. This is what makes people go to the gym a few times and stop and what sabotages their intentions to learn a new language or a new skill – and you'll discover a right-brain strategy for overcoming the obstacle every time it pops up in your life.

If you've been focusing on your weaknesses rather than your strengths, you've inadvertently been sabotaging your own progress. In Chapter 5 you'll see that putting your attention on your strengths is the secret known by all high-achievers, and find out how you can do it, too.

The biggest enemy of focus is procrastination. If you finally want to overcome it, the answers are in Chapter 6.

If you've ever put off doing the important things because you're not in the right mood, the innovative Alter Ego strategy in Chapter 7 is going to unlock your productivity. This one technique alone has the power to transform your effectiveness the minute you start using it.

While it's important to be focused yourself, of course you also depend on others to cooperate with you. In Chapter 8 you will read how to set boundaries, how to say no, and how to manage other people so they help you reach your goals.

Chapter 9 takes this further with specific techniques of language that reveal why most conversations are dead ends and how to transform them into persuasive communication. You'll learn how to recognise other people's language patterns and use that knowledge to establish greater rapport with them. The additional methods covered include reframing, pacing and leading, and using metaphors and stories.

The next few chapters cover the most powerful enemies of creativity and productivity: information overload (Chapter 10), mountains of paperwork (Chapter 11), the email monster (Chapter 12), endless or irrelevant meetings (Chapter 13) and deadlines and the need to handle multiple projects (Chapter 14). For each of these you will discover new solutions.

Zooming ahead in your career can be stressful as well as rewarding so Chapter 15 shows you how to stay calm, relaxed and flexible so that you can stay in a state of focus.

Finally, in Chapter 16 you'll see how to put all of this into a plan of action. It recaps the key points of all the chapters that have gone before and guides you through the process of achieving your goal. You can use this plan again and again as you set new goals for yourself in any area of your life.

Because there are some resources I wanted to share with you that don't fit within the pages of a book, I've also set up the www.focusquick.com website. There you will find chapter bonuses such as audio guided visualisations you can download and take with you on your MP3 player, video interviews with experts on communication and productivity, and much more.

You are about to embark on a great adventure – the adventure of finally achieving the success you have been waiting for and you deserve. Let's get started!

Part

1

Finding your focus

1

How to focus on your vital 20%

What if I told you that you have it within your power to turbo-charge your life, to get more done, make more money, and enjoy more success, just by focusing more of your time and energy doing more of some of what you already do? It's true, and it's based on a well-known principle that has been around for over a century. However, there is a simple and hidden obstacle that stops most people from ever implementing it. It's as though there's a great cave of treasure, with the opening easy to see, the sparkling gems and gold beckoning, but only one in a thousand individuals steps in and helps themselves.

This chapter will tell you what this principle is and how it works in your life, and the rest of the book will give you the tools and techniques you need in order to overcome the obstacles that keep most people at a mediocre level of achievement because they never put this principle into practice. I guarantee that if you apply this principle consistently, it will change your life dramatically for the better.

Business management thinker Joseph M. Juran suggested the principle and named it after Italian economist Vildredo Pareto, who observed that 80% of income in Italy went to 20% of the population. He then carried out surveys on a number of other countries and found that a similar distribution applied (in some countries, the wealth is concentrated in an even smaller percentage of individuals). Eventually his observation became a common rule of thumb in business; e.g., "80% of your sales come from 20% of your clients."

Pareto's Principle

At some point, you may already have run across the 80/20 rule, also known as Pareto's Principle. It says that 80% of your profits or value come from only 20% of your efforts.

The average office worker can easily verify this. Out of each eight-hour day, probably only an hour and a half is spent doing things that really pay off. That's the 20%, and it might involve making decisions about a new product or service, setting new priorities or goals, directing others in their work, and so on. The other 80% of the time might include such low-value activities as sorting through your e-mail, sitting in on meetings that don't directly concern you but that it seems politic to attend, taking care of minor but urgent matters, fending off salespeople whose products or services aren't appropriate for you, and on phone calls that are more social chats than business.

Are there colleagues who take up 80% of your time but give you less than 20% of value (however you define it)? It's time to ration their access to you and give more time to those who contribute more value.

The same rule often applies to products. Many companies offer a large range of items, but if they analyse where their profits come from, they find that it's from a relatively small number of items. This may be because those items sell in the largest quantities, or because they have the largest mark-up.

Service businesses may have a large number of clients, but they find that most of their profits come from a relative few. They probably also find that 20% of their clients or customers account for 80% of the time-consuming questions, minor complaints and last-minute changes. What's more, the 20% who provide the most value usually are *not* the same 20% who create the most problems. Businesses that have "fired" their most difficult clients often find that it frees them up to make more money, not to mention the reduction in stress and aggravation.

The principle even applies in some aspects of your home life. Most likely you wear 20% of your wardrobe 80% of the time, and about 20% of your carpet gets 80% of the wear. Eighty per cent of your arguments with your spouse or partner are probably caused by 20% of the total topics about which you disagree (for most couples, these are money, who does the domestic chores, and issues about child-raising).

Eliminate the power of the negative 20%

So far we've been looking at actions that result in positive outcomes, but the 80/20 principle applies to the negative as well. For example, about 20% of criminals commit 80% of crimes. This is why New York's "zero tolerance" policy was effective – it turns out that the people who were taken off the streets for committing minor crimes were also the ones who had been committing major crimes.

A common negative business example: one encounter with a rude or clueless customer service representative may amount to a very small portion of our interaction with a company and its products, yet it can be enough to colour our entire perception.

In our personal lives, sometimes what we do 20% of the time, or less, creates 80% of our unhappiness. For instance, someone might spend a small amount of time picking fights with their spouse, but it might contribute a large proportion of their unhappiness the rest of the time.

Naturally, in the case of negative actions, we would seek to reduce the 20% instead of increasing it. In most cases, though, the best strategy is to spend so much time doing the things that give us positive results that they drive out the negative ones anyway. People who are leading truly productive, enjoyable lives usually lose interest in the negative activities in which they used to indulge.

Why it's important to focus on the positive

Kathryn D. Cramer, a psychologist who has written the book, *Change the Way You See Everything*, points out that 80% of the time we tend to be alert for what's not working, whereas research has shown that focusing on what we do well is the key to accelerating progress. Why do we focus on the negative? Because we are trained to. She points out that up until we are three or four years old, just about anything we do is greeted with applause and appreciation by the adults in our lives. But when we get to school, the focus changes to what we are doing wrong, and it stays that way right through further education.

You can choose what you think about, and it is far more productive to focus 80% of your thinking on your strengths, on what is working well in your life, and what the potential is in other areas.

If you are used to emphasising the negative, it can take a while to change that habit, but there are ways you can help move yourself to a more positive orientation:

- Every morning when you wake up, take a minute or two to remind yourself of the things in your life for which you are grateful. Also think about the things you are looking forward to that day.

- Throughout the day, when something goes well, take a moment to register it. These do not have to be major achievements. For example, it might just be a phone call that you handled skilfully or a question you were able to answer for a colleague. This may sound trivial, but how many trivial negative things do you normally notice in a day? By noticing the good ones, you restore a balance in your thinking.

- Also notice what other people are doing that is positive and beneficial and take the time to compliment them for it. Bad managers tend to note only the times when a subordinate gets it wrong. Good managers know that the best way to train people is to reinforce effective behaviour.

- At night, briefly go over the events of the day. For both the positive and negative, consider what you learned from them. If something did go badly, how will you handle a similar situation next time? The personal development saying that "there are no mistakes, only learning experiences", may sound naïve, but there is an element of truth to it as well.

This change in your way of thinking may in fact be the most important aspect of implementing the 80/20 rule, because it's difficult to change negative behaviour without first changing negative attitudes.

Let's have a look at how much scope there is in your work life for turbo-charging your career with a shift to the most valuable 20%.

What is your positive 20% to focus on at work?

Take a moment to think about how the 80/20 rule applies to you in your work life. What's the most productive thing you do in your work week?

Now estimate how much of your time you spend actually doing that one thing. I've put this question to executives, artists, a children's entertainer, teachers, doctors – and generally they have said they spend only from 10 to 20% doing the most productive tasks. Naturally that means the majority of their time is spent on things that produce less value. Here's the fact that reveals why so many people never go beyond the average: most of us are wasting our valuable time.

The implications of the 80/20 rule are simple, and they apply right across the board: if you can spend more of your time on your key 20% of activities, you'll be much more productive (and, most likely, make more money).

> You can apply the 80/20 principle to your work environment. Are the things you need 80% of the time (e.g., stapler, current project folders, tape, etc.) within your reach, or is your desk cluttered with things you use less than 20% of the time? Rearrange the items as necessary.

The process is also simple: identify your top 20% of activities and do more of them, which means, of course, doing fewer of the not-so-profitable 80%. Later we'll look at the best ways to get rid of those less valuable activities.

❝identify your top 20% of activities and do more of them❞

The first step is looking at what you're doing now. Below, write the 10 tasks or activities that take most of your time at work. Naturally these will vary depending on what you do for a living but examples might include writing reports, attending meetings, make sales phone calls, or checking the internet for relevant news. Don't go by your job description or what you intend to do, but what actually takes up your work time.

The 10 tasks that currently take up most of your work time

1. _____ (%)

2. _____ (%)

3. _____ (%)

4. _____ (%)

5 _____ (%)

6. _____ (%)

7. _____ (%)

8. _____ (%)

9. _____ (%)

10. _____ (%)

Now go back and jot down by each item what percentage of your total work time you dedicate to each of the 10 work tasks you've listed. If you do a lot more than 10 kinds of things, the total will not add up to 100%, nor do you have to be a perfectionist about getting each percentage right, you can just take an educated guess. If you want to be more precise, you can use a calculator. If, for example, you work 40 hours a week and you spend three of those on the first task, you'd divide 3 by 40 and the result would show that you spend 7.5% on that task.

Now in the spaces opposite, write down the three things you do at work that add the most value – that is, bring in the most money, or represent the biggest contribution that you make. These may already be on your list above, or it may be that one or more of them didn't make your top 10 list because you spend so little time on them.

The three tasks that add the most value at work

1. _____ (%)

2. _____ (%)

3. _____ (%)

Now estimate how much of your time you spend on these three. Ideally the three that are most valuable are also the ones that take up the three biggest chunks of your work time, but that rarely is the case. Don't worry, though, a bit later you'll see how you can change your time use in a way that will drastically accelerate your success.

What is your top 20% to focus on at leisure?

Now let's look at how Pareto's Principle plays out in your personal life by making a similar list of how you spend your leisure time. Below, jot down the 10 (or fewer) things on which you spend the most time when you're not working (don't include sleeping and eating). Again, these will vary greatly from person to person, but may include watching TV, reading, playing sports or exercising, or going to the movies. Only list the things that you actually do; for example, you may be interested in the theatre or going to museums, but unless they are in the top 10 uses of your leisure time, don't include them.

The 10 activities that currently take up most of your free time:

1. _____ (%)
2. _____ (%)
3. _____ (%)
4. _____ (%)
5. _____ (%)
6. _____ (%)
7. _____ (%)
8. _____ (%)
9. _____ (%)
10. _____ (%)

As before, estimate what percentage of your leisure time each of these takes.

Then jot down below the three activities that give you the most enjoyment. If there are any you believe would be very satisfying but they're not on the list above, add them.

The three free-time activities that add the most enjoyment:

1. _____ (%)
2. _____ (%)
3. _____ (%)

Now estimate what percentage of your total free time you spend on each of these three. In their personal lives, too, most people will find that the three on which they spend the most time are not the three they enjoy most.

> If you want more information on Pareto's Principle, entrepreneur and management consultant Richard Koch has written three books on its applications: *The 80/20 Principle*, *The 80/20 Individual*, and *Living the 80/20 Way*.

Why we stick with unsatisfying tasks or activities

You may find that several items on your list take a fair amount of your spare time, yet they're not that enjoyable. These are things we do out of habit or because we think someone else expects us to do them. Often we delay doing things that we believe would give us greater pleasure on the basis that we'll get to them someday. That might be, "When the kids are older", or "When I retire", or "When we've saved up enough money." Unfortunately, in many cases that someday never comes.

Another factor is the "good money after bad" phenomenon. Studies of decision-making reveal that the more you invest in something (in terms of money, time, or emotions), the more commitment you feel toward it. For example, if you've read 200 pages of a 300-page book and are bored by it, you may feel that you should finish it anyway because you've come this far. The same effect applies to investments that you should dump or things you've bought that no longer serve you ("I can't throw it out or sell it for a small amount – it cost me so much to buy!").

A good strategy for overcoming this is to apply the "zero-base" criterion. Ask yourself: "If I had not yet bought this (or committed to spend time on this) – would I?" If not, it may be time to stop, dump, or sell!

Another factor may be pride. If you've announced to the world that you're going to participate in a marathon and then you find out that all that running is causing pain and damage to your knees, you may not quit even though stopping is in the best interests of your health. A good way to deal with this is to take a step back and see the situation more objectively. If a friend were in this situation, what would you advise? Most likely you'd say, "Don't be silly, your health is more important than anything else", and that's your answer for yourself as well.

In this chapter you have clarified what aspects of your work and leisure life have the potential to increase hugely your levels of prosperity and happiness. In the next chapter, you'll learn exactly how to focus these elements into specific goals and the secret that will help you reach the goals you set.

Website chapter bonus

At www.focusquick.com you'll find an audio interview with entrepreneur Yaro Starak with his thoughts about how to apply the 80/20 principle for maximum results.

2

CHAPTER TWO
How to focus on your first goals

In the previous chapter you found out that the secret of getting massive results is to figure out the 20% of your work or your leisure time that gives you the greatest benefit, and to spend more time doing that, and less time doing the 80% of things that give you less value. Once you know what that vital 20% is, you can set goals that will speed you toward success. But if you've tried setting goals in the past you may find this a discouraging prospect because you don't yet know the two fatal flaws in most goal-setting approaches. In this chapter, you're about to find out not only what these flaws are, but also how to overcome them.

How to set SMART goals

Focusing requires being specific about what you want to achieve, which is where SMART goals come in. First, let's look at the process of setting goals, then you can apply it to the areas you identified in the last chapter.

What are SMART goals? S stands for Specific. Goals like "lose some weight" or "make more money" or "be more popular" aren't very useful because they are so vague; if you lose one ounce, you've lost weight but aren't likely to be satisfied, so it makes sense to set a specific weight target. The same applies to money and even to a personal quality like being more popular. What, exactly, would being more popular look like? Does it mean having two more close friends? Or having another half a dozen casual friends? If you have trouble coming up with specifics, just ask yourself, what will you see and hear when the goal has been reached, that is different from what you see and hear now?

When you make these decisions be sure that you are using criteria that are meaningful to you, not ones you think other people expect from you. Trying to fulfil someone else's expectations is a fool's errand, not least because if we do happen to fulfil them, they can be changed in an instant to something else that will keep us struggling.

It's also better to be positive – so rather than having the goal of "losing 10 pounds", it would be better to "achieve a healthy weight of X." Otherwise you will constantly have your mind on the negative.

M stands for Measurable. Once you have been specific, the way to measure whether or not you have reached the goal usually is implied. If it's about weight, you'll use the scales or a bodyfat monitor; if it's about money, your bank balance will tell the tale. In fact, whether or not you can measure it is a good test of whether you have been specific enough. If not, go back and adjust the goal.

The next two goals, A and R, are for Attainable and Realistic. I'm not a big fan of emphasising these too much. Goals need to be ambitious and glorious if they're going to motivate you to do the work necessary to reach them, and the most exciting goals tend to be the ones you're not 100% sure are attainable and realistic. Can your book become a best-seller even though you've never written one before? Can you start a business that makes enough money within the next five years to allow you to stop working and devote yourself to your hobby or to charitable work? Well, lots of people have done those. And there's only one way to find out: write the book or start the business and see what happens.

The only real question is whether the sacrifices you are willing to make match the scope of the goal. If the answer is yes, go for it. If you give it your all, you'll probably get there.

By the way, if you want to consult someone about whether to embark on your big plans, please ask someone who has done it, not someone who hasn't. The former is an expert on how it can be done, the latter is an expert on how it can't be done.

The T in SMART is for Timely, which usually is interpreted to mean that you have to have a deadline for reaching the goal. This is the one that destroys a lot of hopes and plans.

Beware the deadly deadline

Here's the way it usually goes: you set a goal with a deadline, something like, "I will weigh 10 stone by March 1st", or "I will get an agent to represent my book by the end of September", or "I will start my new internet-based business by February 15th."

Then you do whatever you think will allow you to reach the goal by your deadline or target date. And, if you're like most of us, quite often you fail. Either you actually gain weight, or you stay the same, or you lose some weight but don't reach the target. Or you don't get an agent by the end of September, and because of a problem with your website, your online business isn't actually ready to go by mid-February.

You've failed, and when we fail we feel disappointed or depressed and we're likely to give up on the goal. Furthermore, we are a bit less likely to try to reach another goal in the future.

There are two fatal weaknesses in this traditional approach to setting goals. The first is setting the deadline. The self-development gurus would be aghast at that statement. They say that a goal without a deadline is just a wish. To that I would say, often a goal *with* a deadline is a prescription for failure. Here's why: when you set out to reach a goal, generally you don't yet know how you're going to do it. You may have some idea about the strategies you will use and the tasks you will implement, but you can't know whether or how well it will work. The second flaw is that in many cases reaching the goal requires the cooperation of other people. You can influence their responsiveness but not control it. Therefore, how can you possibly set a time limit for success?

There is only one true goal deadline

Above, I mentioned how the process usually goes. Here is how it should go, if you really want to achieve the goal:

1. You set the goal. For our example, we'll stick with reaching a target weight.
2. You do whatever you think will get you there. Let's say that you decide to walk a mile three times a week in order to burn up calories, with the intention of losing one pound per week.

3. You monitor how well the process is working. If what you're doing gives you the results you want (e.g., you find you're a pound per week closer to your goal), you just keep doing it until you reach your goal.

4. If what you're doing isn't giving you the results you want, you brainstorm alternatives and commit to doing something different. This may be just a small adjustment, or it may be a total change of strategy. For instance, you might find that you're losing only a tiny amount of weight, so you decide that in addition to the extra walking, you will have only fresh fruit for snacks and dessert. Or you may decide that you will try working out with a personal trainer twice a week.

5. Repeat steps 3 and 4 until you reach the goal. Your deadline becomes "whenever I have achieved what I set out to achieve". Your commitment is just to keep on doing something different, until you find what works. With some goals you'll get there fast, with others it will take longer. But with this approach there is no failure, only a learning process.

I want to repeat for emphasis: in this approach, *there is no failure*! The only way you could fail would be to give up.

This also helps you avoid the "faster and more" syndrome. That happens when a deadline approaches and the methods you are using aren't working very well. The impulse is to try to meet the deadline by doing whatever you're doing faster and/or doing more of it. But doing more of what doesn't work, or doing it faster, obviously isn't really the answer. Without the pressure of the deadline, you are more likely to be open to considering alternative strategies.

THE STUDY THAT NEVER WAS

Many self-deveopment books include the story of a study that was done at Harvard (or sometimes they say Yale) back in the '50s, in which students were asked whether they had written goals. Thirty years later, the 3% who said yes had earned more than the other 97% put together. The only problem is that the study never existed. No one is sure how the story got started, but there is no evidence that such a survey ever took place. However, many successful people do say they had written goals.

This doesn't mean that you can't set deadlines for **tasks** under your control within the goal. For example, if your goal is to find someone to design your website for your new internet business, you can resolve to research candidates and contact the top three by the end of the week. If your goal is to find an agent, you can write to three of them by tomorrow. If you decide to work out at a gym, you can set yourself the deadline of joining one by Monday.

Grand goals are great but break them into chunks

Grand goals pull you forward into the future you want for yourself. At the same time, it's important to break them down into smaller chunks that allow you to have a continual feeling of progress and achievement. Don't put off celebrating until you reach the ultimate goal. Establish milestones and celebrate those as well.

Planning is good, doing is better

The steps of the process require a little planning on your part, but beware of getting caught up in the fun of planning to the exclusion of actually taking action. If you love coming up with elaborate plans, diagrams, flow charts, mind maps, etc. (I know whereof I speak), consider cutting back on the planning and putting more attention on achieving. By all means, use charts and other visual aids to help you focus on what you need to do, but make sure they re not a substitute for actually doing the tasks. In business, the two parts of the process are referred to as planning the work and working the plan.

The fact that things are changing more quickly than ever also means that we have to be more flexible. These days, having a five-year plan that we consider set in stone is not realistic. You have to be ready to pay attention to clues along the way that might point you in a better direction, either about where you're going or how to get there.

There's a good analogy for this in an experiment conducted in the field of art. The work of two sets of skilled art students was compared. The first set knew the outcome they wanted, planned it carefully, and moved toward it step by step, with minimal changes. The second group had only a rough idea of what they were going for, and they changed their designs an average of 17 times. At the end, judges evaluated the two sets of paintings, and found the second set to be more creative. The lesson is that leaving enough flexibility for variation and experimentation will give you better results.

Your strategy for persistence

So far, so good. But there is a second hidden obstacle that you need to overcome. Often we commit to a strategy (e.g., go walking three times a week) and we do well keeping it up for the first week or even the first month. Then life gets in the way and we find that we're going only once a week, or not at all. The outcome: failure. Every gym counts on this. In January, lots of people sign up for an annual membership (the effect of New Year's resolutions) but by March most of the new members stop showing up. Great if you're the gym, not so great if you're the member!

We need not only a strategy for reaching a goal, we also need a strategy for making sure that we follow through with our own strategy. As I said above, the only way you can fail is if you stop. But often we do stop implementing the strategy. As soon as you notice that happening, you can implement Plan B:

❝the only way you can fail is if you stop❞

1. Decide whether you stopped because it wasn't working after you'd given it a fair trial. If yes, then it's time to brainstorm a new strategy and implement that one. The same is true if you stopped because whatever you were doing is too hard to implement. For example, maybe you resolved to go to the gym seven days a week, but you're finding that this isn't realistic. You could decide that you'll go three days a week, and see how that works.

2. If you stopped just because you forgot, or it was inconvenient, or you got lazy, then it's time to brainstorm a strategy for how you can make it easier, more pleasant, and more likely to be on your mind. In our example, this could be by

finding a workout buddy, or hiring a personal trainer, or promising to give your teenager a sum of money every time you miss your appointment at the gym.

> By considering a temporary failure as just a step toward eventual success, you remove its stigma. If you find this difficult, take an inventory of the skills you have now, in every part of your life. Then consider how many mis-steps or learning experiences you had on the way to mastering these skills. Most likely you will have to think hard, because once we reach a goal we tend to forget the obstacles we overcame in the process. That will also be the case when you have reached the goals that may at the moment seem distant.

You can't focus on what you don't see

Studies have shown that you are likely to snack more when sweets are in a transparent container than in an opaque one, and when the container is within easy reach than when you have to get up to get to it. These results are not exactly earth-shaking, but they do remind us of an important principle: namely, out of sight, out of mind (as well as "in sight, in mind").

If you want to be sure to spend time every day working on something that is important to you, keep a symbol of it visible or audible. This could be a photo or drawing, a word or a phrase, or a piece of music. It helps to change this symbol periodically to refresh its power to remind you to take action.

Time to focus on your top three goals

With this understanding of how goal-setting really works, you're ready to set your own top goals. Look back at your

80/20 lists, give some thought to what goals you would find most exciting and fulfilling, and then write down the three that you would most like to achieve:

Goal 1. _____

Goal 2. _____

Goal 3. _____

Which of these are you ready to commit to, starting right now? You can choose one, two, or all three. If you can tell that doing all three would be extremely time-consuming, then start with just one or two. Succeeding at one will give you greater energy and satisfaction than struggling to achieve three at the same time. If you do want to go for more than one, it helps if they're not all in the same sector of your life. For instance, you might choose one goal that relates to your career, one that relates to fitness and health, and one that is about improving an important relationship.

For each of the goals get a nice notebook that you will enjoy writing in. You can use the blanks and forms in this book, but you'll also want more space to record all the actions you take, the milestones you pass, the strategies that work really well and that you can apply in the future to other goals, and so on.

Start with these questions

For the goal that you consider most important, answer the questions below (if you need more space, use your notebook). For our examples, let's say that you realised in your 80/20 evaluation that you make the most money doing design work, but your lack of expertise in using the Photoshop software program is holding you back. One of your goals could be to acquire those skills.

1. Identify what the situation is like now. Be as specific as possible.

   (*Example: I bought Photoshop instructional DVDs but have never used them.*)

2. What did you do (or not do) that is responsible for how this situation is now?

   (*Example: I never scheduled time to learn the program.*)

3. What will you do differently in order to get the outcome you want?

   (*Example: I will spend four hours a week learning the program.*)

4. What do you need to have or do in order to be sure that you can actually do what you have specified in the previous step?

   (*Example: I have to decide what I'm doing for four hours a week currently that I will replace with four hours of learning.*)

5. What resources (time, money, help from others) do you need? How will you get them? Is there anything you need to give up or stop doing in order to free these resources?

   (*Example: The resource I need is time. I will cut back by four hours a week on watching TV. I also need to put in place a system that reminds me to do the lessons.*)

6. Do the different things and conduct an ongoing evaluation of whether they are working. If not, consider what you might do differently to get the results you want. Keep doing this until you have reached the goal.

   (*Example: If you find yourself consistently unable to spend four focused hours at home learning the program, you might want to consider taking your laptop to a library or other place where you won't be interrupted. Or you may find that self-instruction doesn't work so well for you and that it would be better to do a course.*)

If you want to commit to more than one goal, answer the same questions for each one.

Rev up your passion with a Top Ten list

Particularly if your goal is an ambitious one, you may feel daunted by the prospect of starting to aim for it. Maybe you're familiar with talk show host David Letterman's *Top Ten List*. You can adapt it to get yourself off to a rousing start. Make up a list of the top ten reasons why you believe each goal is important to your future, or why you really want to achieve it. This list will help motivate you if you run out of steam along the way. It can even be useful to make up big Top Ten posters to display in your office or meeting room, to remind yourself of these key motivations. Try this now for one of your goals:

Top ten reasons I want to achieve this goal

10. _____

9. _____

8. _____

7. _____

6. _____

5. _____

4. _____

3. _____

2. _____

1. _____

> If you find your motivation faltering, put your Top Ten list on a slip of paper and carry it with you in your wallet or purse and review it frequently. It may also be a useful antidote to the ease with which other people come up with reasons why your goal will be hard to reach. Most people's default setting is negativity, so being ready to counter it will help you.

See yourself as the hero you are

Another great way to gain confidence in your ability to reach your goal is using the hero's journey as a template for your actions. The idea of the hero's journey stems from the work of Joseph Campbell, who was one of the world's foremost students of mythology. He found that in many cultures there were myths that had basically the same structure: a hero going on a quest.

Along the way the hero finds a mentor, but the mentor can go along for only part of the journey, and then the hero has to proceed alone. He faces various tests and challenges, and goes deeply into the world of his adventure.

At some point he confronts the greatest challenge and may despair of succeeding or even surviving. At this stage, he discovers a new strength or sense of purpose, and he goes on to triumph.

Often the treasure the hero wins is symbolic – that is, something real like a gem or golden goblet that also represents some new knowledge or wisdom he has gained as a result of his journey. Sometimes this treasure benefits not only the hero but also the people around him or even his whole tribe or country.

If this pattern sounds familiar, that's not surprising, because it is a story structure also used in many novels and films. George Lucas used it for his first three *Star Wars* movies and struck up a friendship with Campbell.

Even more interesting, though, is that it is a pattern that fits many of our real-life adventures. When I conduct my *Create Your Future* workshop, I invite participants first to use this structure to describe how they have handled a challenge in the past, for example, going to college, starting a career, or learning a new skill. Often, people are surprised to realise they've been heroes.

Then I ask them to use this structure to describe how they could accomplish something they haven't done yet. The result is always interesting and sometimes profound. Not only is the hero's journey a useful planning tool, but the effect of thinking of ourselves as heroes and heroines on a journey of adventure can have a fantastic motivational effect. Switching from "I have a problem" or even "I have a goal" to "I am on a quest" is a big shift.

Try it yourself with one of your big goals. Fill in the blanks below, and whenever you're not sure of what the answer is, just take a guess. If you relax and let answers come to you, you may be surprised that your subconscious mind offers up more about this journey than you knew you knew.

Your heroic journey

1. The hero is introduced in his ordinary world. (What are you doing now, just before you embark on your heroic journey?)

_____

_____

Frank may have taken the hero's journey idea one step too far.

2. The call to adventure. (What is the thing that made you realise that you have a problem or challenge or that you want to start a new adventure?)

_____

_____

3. The hero is reluctant at first, and has fear of the unknown. (What is your greatest fear about embarking on this new adventure?)

_____

_____

4. The hero is encouraged by The Wise Old Man or Wise Old Woman. (Who is your mentor or role model who can give you some kind of guidance or inspiration? It can be a real person from the past or present, or even a character from fiction.)

_____

_____

5. The hero passes the first threshold and fully enters the world of the new story. (At what point will you make – or did you make – a full commitment to your adventure?)

_____

_____

6. The hero encounters tests and helpers. (What do you think will be some of the early challenges you will face? Who can give you support and help?)

_____

_____

7. The hero reaches the innermost cave – a dangerous place. (What do you think will be the point of greatest challenge – a time you might ordinarily have considered giving up?)

_____

_____

8. The hero endures the supreme ordeal, appears to die and be born again. (What quality will allow you to survive the greatest challenge? What will be the signal of your rebirth?)

_____

_____

9. The hero seizes the sword and takes possession of the treasure. (What is the treasure you will win? It could be knowledge and experience or something more tangible.)

_____

_____

10. The road back and the chase. (Once you have reached your goal, what smaller difficulties might still need to be overcome?)

_____

_____

11. The hero returns with the treasure back to the ordinary world. (What will be different in your world when you have achieved the goal? How will it affect others in your circle?)

_____

_____

JOSEPH CAMPBELL (1904–1987)

was a professor of mythology, writer, and orator. His books include _The Hero With a Thousand Faces_ and the four-volume _The Masks of God_, but the general public became aware of him via his series of interviews with Bill Moyers, called _The Power of Myth_. It was first broadcast on PBS in the US in 1987, the year after Campbell's death, and has been repeated many times as well as being available on DVD.

Your visual focus: map your goals

This next step is the creation of a goal map on which you plot all the major steps toward your goal. If it's a big goal, you will want to break it down into a series of additional maps for sub-goals. For example, let's say that your big goal is to be a publicly-recognised expert on marketing, with at least £100,000 a year coming from several streams of income. The steps to that goal might include writing articles on marketing, becoming a polished public speaker, training to be a business coach, writing a book on marketing, creating a website, and marketing yourself.

> The goal maps in this chapter were created with a software program called Inspiration (see www.inspiration.com). Another program you might like is called Goal Enforcer (see www.goalenforcer.com). Another mind-mapping program, this one free, is Freemind (see www.freemind.sourceforge.net).

The goal map at the top of the facing page indicates these steps in brief form (you'd also want to work out more specific versions). Maps like this are usually organised clockwise, starting at the top right. So in this case, your first task would to write articles, the next would be to become a good speaker, and so forth (although, of course, some of these would actually overlap). While this chapter has emphasised not getting too hung up on deadlines, in this case most of the steps are within your control so you could attach some target dates or time frames.

You can also treat each of the steps toward that big goal as a project, and create a project map for each one. A sample for the step "Become a Good Speaker" is shown below the "Marketing Expert" map, with the first task being "Join Toastmasters", the next, "Have session with a voice coach." Again you could add dates and more detail.

Time to draw your goal map

Your turn. Whether you use software or just draw the map on a sheet of paper with pen or pencil, rough out a goal map for the goal that excites you the most. You can harvest all the information that you came up with in this chapter to help you plot out the key sub-goals you will need to achieve in order to

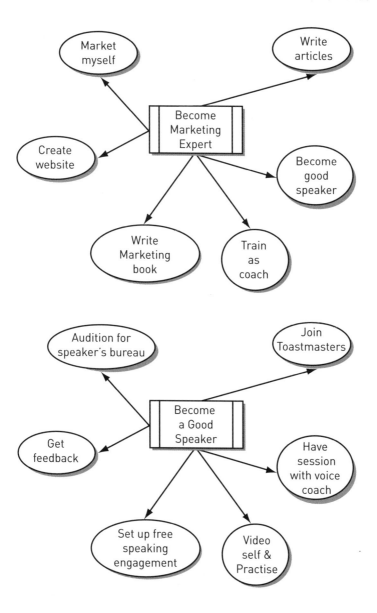

reach the main goal. Then, as you continue to work through the book, draw goal maps for each of these sub-goals, being more and more specific about exactly what you need to do, how, and when. If you prefer, you can read the rest of the book and then do your goal maps as part of the final chapter, "Putting it all together", but I highly recommend doing at least a rough version now.

By identifying one or more of your goals and understanding how to overcome the usual flaws in goal-setting, you have taken a crucial first step in bringing a laser-like focus to your trip toward success. In the next chapter you'll learn how to change your time patterns so they totally support your progress.

Website chapter bonus

At www.focusquick.com you'll find an audio "future inter-view" guided visualisation. By imagining what things will be like when you have achieved your goal, and in your imagin-ation answering a few questions, you will get important clues about the best way to move forward.

Part

2

Your focus strategies

3

How to focus your time patterns for success

In the previous chapter you committed to at least one major goal and discovered how to avoid the typical pitfalls of goal-setting. By putting your focus on goals that have a major potential to change your life for the better, you will be directing all of your efforts to what matters most. However, it may be that you have old habits of how you use your time that are not ideal for speeding you toward success.

In this chapter, you'll learn how to recognise patterns that may be holding you back and how to establish new, more productive patterns. First, a few basic points that will give you the context for these techniques.

The surprising facts about time patterns

1. Everybody has patterns of behaviour. Not surprisingly, doing the same thing again and again results in the same outcomes again and again. For example, someone may keep having different relationships but always with the same kind of person, or someone may repeatedly get into money problems by misusing credit cards. Of course there are also positive patterns. You may know people who

always land a good job or always drive safely. People have certain patterns for how they use their time, too. For instance, some people will always tackle first the task they think will be easiest, while others always start with the one they think will be most difficult.

2. More surprisingly, people tend to repeat their old patterns even when the outcomes aren't positive. In other words, people don't necessarily learn from their bad experiences that maybe it would be a good idea to do something different (a little later we'll look at why this is). Therefore, it's not unusual for people to use inefficient or unproductive time patterns for years.

3. People tend to be aware of other people's patterns, but not their own. It's unlikely that we will change until we are aware of our patterns. Once we do know what they are, it becomes easier to change them, and therefore to change the outcomes.

4. Patterns can include feelings, thoughts, and images as well as actions. For example, if you request a pay rise and don't get it, the next step may be to remember all the other rejections you've had. Then you might remember the voice of some negative adult from your childhood telling you that you'll never amount to anything. Then you might picture getting rejections in the future for a project you're currently working on, and then it might seem that the best way to blot out all these negative thoughts and feelings is to go to the pub. That's a disempowering pattern. An empowering one might be to hear the rejection, remember other times when something that was initially rejected went on to be accepted, ask for feedback on what to do differently in order to get a salary increase next time, and then do that (or consider looking for a different job if there is no chance of advancement in your present one).

How to discover your own patterns

Here are the most common general dysfunctional patterns:

- Get-in-shape *déjà vu* (sign up for gym, go for a week, quit).
- Serial job dissatisfaction.
- Continuous financial discontent.
- Repetitive toxic relationships.

And here are some of the most common dysfunctional patterns relating to time use:

- Doing the least important work first.
- Procrastination.
- "Fire fighting" (doing what is urgent rather than what is important).
- Letting the inner critic dominate thoughts.

It's pretty easy to see that people who have these patterns will be easily distracted from reaching their goals.

How can we open our eyes to our own patterns? First, let's be clear why we're doing this: so we can figure out what we can do differently in order to get better results. With that in mind, here are six different approaches to discovering your own patterns:

1. Ask other people. We can see their faults, so guess what? They can see ours. But you have to convince them that you want them to be honest, and you have to be sure that you can hear this kind of blunt honesty without endangering your relationship. It may be uncomfortable, but you're doing it so you can move forward. If several people recognise the same pattern in your life, they're probably right. Good questions to ask include, "What do you notice about

how I use time? What are the ways you may have noticed me wasting time? When do you think I'm best at it?" If there's nobody you feel comfortable asking this kind of question, ask them of yourself and jot down the answers.

2. Consider what negative patterns your parents had and assess whether you may be duplicating them. It could also be that as part of your rebellion against your parents, you took on a pattern that is the opposite of theirs but that is also negative (e.g., "Trust no one"/"Trust everyone"). In terms of time use, your parents may have had the pattern of putting things off until they turned into emergencies, or they may have been such perfectionists that they never had time to do all they wanted to do. If so, how do you think this has affected your ideas about using time?

3. Think about a situation in which you'd like to understand your behaviour better. Imagine seeing yourself in that situation as though it's playing on a movie screen with you as one of the actors who can be observed. This is the *dissociated state*, as opposed to the *associated state* of seeing things through your own eyes. If you are truly dissociated, you won't have any particular feelings about what you're observing – no guilt, embarrassment, or anything else. You're just watching to find out what you can about this pattern. For example, if you have started and then abandoned learning a new skill in the past, review exactly what happened.

4. Use the "teach your problem" technique. In this, you pretend you have to teach someone how to behave the way you do. You have to give them exact, detailed instructions. For example, let's say the situation you're looking at is why you never seem to catch up paying the bills on the weekends, even though that's always your intention. To

teach someone how to do this, you might instruct them to make promises to their spouse, partner, or children that involve activities that take up most of the weekend. You might teach them to let minor tasks go during the week, so by the weekend they absolutely need to be done. You might instruct them to stay up late on Friday and Saturday nights, so they don't actually get up until noon on Saturday and Sunday. You can write down this detailed curriculum, or you can dictate it into a tape recorder, or if you're brave you can do it with another person being the "student" and let them take notes for you. You will have a list of behaviours that you can change one by one.

5. The next time you go through a pattern, map it as you go. For example, let's say you are working at home on Friday and intend to use that time write a report. Friday comes around but by the end of the day you still didn't get the report done. As it happens, make notes about the process that causes you to change your mind. For example, maybe you get up and notice that the laundry has really piled up. You decide to put it into the washing machine and then write the report. But as the washing is being done, you

think that you might as well quickly give your home office a quick once-over to tidy it up so that you'll really be able to concentrate on your writing. Just as you finish and are ready to sit down at your desk, a friend phones. She's upset and needs a shoulder to cry on, so you sit there and listen to her latest romantic misadventure for an hour. Now you're hungry so you make yourself a late lunch – after all, you can't write well if you are hungry … and so it goes. (Note: writing down a pattern as it happens often is enough of a pattern-interruption that it will cause you to go ahead with what you originally intended – so this can be a curative exercise as well as a diagnostic one.)

6. Use the "letter from your higher self" technique. For something that you'd like to change, sit quietly and ask your higher self for some insights into your current main time patterns. By "higher self" I don't mean anything too mystical, just the part of you that is detached from the stresses of the moment and seems to know what is best. Write down anything that occurs to you, without worrying about whether or not it's really coming from your higher self. Some people find that they get better insights if they write things down with the "wrong" hand (that is, the one they normally don't write with). You may find that in this process your higher self not only diagnoses the problems but also jumps ahead to possible solutions.

Start now by jotting down below at least three patterns that you have that are not supporting your most valuable and focused use of your time. When you've done a bit more digging, you can add more.

Time patterns that do not serve you well:

1. _____

2. _____

3. _____

4. _____

5. _____

6. _____

Understand what your current pattern gives you

One of the assumptions of a very useful psychological approach called Neuro Linguistic Programming is that every behaviour has a positive intention. It's trying to give you some benefit.

The book, *Introducing NLP* by Joseph O'Connor and John Seymour, HarperCollins, 2003, is a good place to start if you're interested in finding out more about NLP.

When you've identified a negative pattern, clarify what it's giving you. Usually it will be some kind of protection, often a protection from needing to face change, which is uncomfortable initially and sometimes very scary indeed. Even though this protection has negative side effects, it's the devil you know. It allows you to keep on doing the things you've learned to do in the past, rather than having to change.

“When you've identified a negative pattern, clarify what it's giving you. ”

Let's look at a few more examples:

- The person who keeps putting off clearing out their "junk room" may be afraid of having to throw away items that have sentimental value and give them comfort. By avoiding the task, they get the pay-off of continuing to draw the solace they get from just knowing the items are there.

- The person who creates something, such as a painting, a manuscript, or an idea for a new business, but never shows it to anyone, may fear the same kind of ridicule they got when they were the overweight kid in the PE class. By never letting anyone judge their work they get the pay-off of avoiding ridicule. Naturally this kind of reaction is unlikely even if the idea or product is bad, but we're not talking about logic here, rather about emotions.

- The person who wants to make a career change but never moves towards it gets the pay-off of not having to risk rejection.

There are some simple patterns that may not have a deep pay-off, they may just be bad habits that you've fallen into. These should be easy to change. However, when you confront a set of behaviours that are not easy to change, it's worth investigating the pay-off. Again, please note that the point of this is not to criticise yourself for your behaviour, but rather to use it as a starting point for change. Write down the top three time patterns that work against your success and then, below each, what pay-off you think it gives you.

Pay-offs of your least effective time patterns

Pattern 1._____

The pay-off. _____

Pattern 2._____

The pay-off. _____

Pattern 3._____

The pay-off. _____

Before you can change your negative patterns into more productive ones, you will have to figure out how to get these pay-offs in other ways.

Find better ways to get a similar pay-off

Let's relate this to the 80/20 patterns. Suppose someone has an idea for an online business he thinks could be very profitable. If he spent 80% of his available time actually implementing his idea, that would probably give him a great deal of value. Instead, he spends 80% or more of his time researching, reading, and learning about online marketing but never actually gets a website, never develops the product or service, never attracts potential customers.

He can rationalise that he needs to get all the latest information available before he takes action, but what do you think might be the real pay-off?

For as long as he is only planning, he can't fail. But we learn by trial and error, and a beautiful plan that is not implemented will never bring in any money. However, simply telling him (or yourself) to get on with it is not likely to work. We have to come up with a way that provides much of the safety of the current pattern while doing something different.

If you're suffering "paralysis by analysis", continually researching and planning but not acting, take the first step that seems to make sense. Then you can look for more information as you need it instead of trying to figure out everything before you start.

When you have identified what the pay-off is, you can generate alternatives for getting the same benefits in more benign ways. If our budding entrepreneur's biggest fear is ridicule from other people, maybe because he's tried and failed at a business scheme before, he doesn't have to tell anyone about it. He can test some of his concepts first, and see how it goes. Once he feels a bit more positive, he can share the information with the most supportive person in his life. If he makes some mistakes, which is almost inevitable, he can learn from them and move forward.

Here's the key point: it's not enough to just change your pattern, you must change it in a way that also gives you the pay-off that was provided by the old pattern. If that element is missing, the new pattern is unlikely to last very long.

The person who avoids clearing out a junk room could consciously choose several items to keep for sentimental or comfort value and get rid of the rest. Or they could put the surplus items into boxes and put them in the attic instead of throwing them away. That way they'd still be there if needed. If they're not needed for a year or two, they may then feel secure enough to throw them out.

The person who fears ridicule for a creative effort can test it first with a supportive friend or colleague.

The person who wants to start a new career but is fearful of failure can break the process down into safer chunks. They may be able to try out their new skills in the context of volunteer work, where there is less pressure. For instance, someone considering becoming an events organiser could initially set up a small function for a charity organisation.

> If you have trouble figuring out what's behind one of your patterns, just ask yourself, "What's the worst thing that could happen if I stop doing this?" Then, to find an alternative, ask, "What else could I do that's more positive, but that would prevent the worst from happening?"

The key is finding what works for you, and it's a trial and error process. Please don't expect that the first thing you try will be the perfect solution. Approach the whole thing in the spirit of play and experimentation. We are social scientists seeking what works – or, if you prefer, we are heroes on our own journeys of learning. You can move another step forward by looking back at your three most negative patterns and their pay-offs, and brainstorming some ways to get the same pay-offs in a way that doesn't require you to keep repeating the negative behaviours. Below, jot down at least one idea for how to do this for each of your three patterns:

Alternative ways of getting the pay-offs of three of your negative time patterns:

Benefit 1._____

Better ways of getting this benefit:

_____

_____

_____

Benefit 2. _____

Better ways of getting this benefit:

_____

_____

_____

Benefit 3. _____

Better ways of getting this benefit:

_____

_____

_____

Let's follow this process through for one of the most common negative time patterns.

How to avoid overcommitting

A typical negative time pattern is overcommitting your time. If you do this, you end up stressed because you have more to do than you can accomplish, so you cut corners and end up delivering a disappointing product or service, or you miss your deadlines and disappoint the people waiting for what you've promised, or you drop one or more projects entirely, which upsets people even more and could result in losing your job or losing clients. By trying to do too much, you fail to focus fully on anything.

If we map this process in order to understand exactly what happens, we discover that when someone asks you to do something, you tend to say yes immediately, or you mentally say yes when you think of a new project yourself – you get to work on it right away, and maybe tell others all about it. Unfortunately, what you *don't* do is consider how this is going

"The best-kept secret of business is that great leaders are nearly always extremely lazy, as well as being capable of bouts of intense work. This is not just a weird coincidence. It is because laziness means time to think; and thinking time leads to good ideas, and good ideas, rather than unthinking toil, gives the edge in the business world today."

Tom Hodgkinson, Co-founder, The Idler *magazine.*

to fit in with everything else you're already committed to achieving.

What's the pay-off of doing this repeatedly, even if you've realised in the past that it generally ends badly? There are two:

- If it's someone else asking you to do something, you may not want to upset or disappoint them, so you just say yes.
- If the project is really appealing, you get so excited by it that you think about it in isolation, rather than in the context of all the things you need to do, and you don't want to miss out on something that could be great.

In each of these cases, the culprit is your imagination. You imagine that the person will be upset. You imagine that the project will be really exciting, and you imagine how disappointing it would be to miss out on something.

Insert a pause

To buy yourself some time to overcome your usual emotional response, take at least a few minutes (or a day, if necessary) to consider whether the new project could fit into your schedule.

If it's your own idea, by all means record it. Jot down all the aspects that come to mind, and make a new folder for it. But do not commit to actually taking action on it for at least a week (unless you have nothing else to do). When you come to decide whether you really want to do this new thing, draw a mind-map of all the projects you are already doing, and consider how much of your time each of these will take. If you have a history of being too optimistic about how quickly you can get something done, add another 25% or 50% to your first estimate.

If you are approached by someone else and you find their idea wonderfully exciting, by all means express your feelings, but tell them that you can't commit this instant. I say, "This sounds really fantastic, but before I can commit to it I need to figure out whether I could give it the time it would require to do a good job. Can I get back to you tomorrow and let you know?" That buys me 24 hours in which to take a look at all the other things I'm doing, instead of getting carried away in the excitement of the moment.

If you realise that taking on the new work would be over-committing yourself, figure out alternative ways to get the pay-offs you used to, now in a way that allows you to say no.

Pay-off 1: Not upsetting or disappointing the person asking you to take on more work.

Alternative: Use your imagination to consider how much more upset they are likely to be if you say yes now and later don't deliver or have to back out. Explain to the other person why you can't take on the project and that doing so would only result in disappointment for both of you. This kind of clear explanation should keep them from having an emotional reaction. If appropriate, suggest someone else for the task.

Pay-off 2: The excitement of thinking how great a new project could be and the desire not to miss out.

Alternative: A new project always seems more exciting because it's fresh and has not yet revealed the obstacles it will entail. Remind yourself that every new project has such stumbling blocks, and imagine what some of them might be for this one. Imagine how upsetting it would be having to do something half-way because you don't have the time to do it properly. That is probably something you want to miss. Also imagine missing out on completing your current work successfully because you are trying to do one more thing. Then imagine how great it will be to accomplish the work to which you are already committed.

As you can see, in each case you're using the same thing – your imagination – but in the alternative scenarios you're using it to recommit to what you're already doing and to avoid adding more than you can handle.

Your next steps

Now that you have worked out some goals and found out how to shift patterns that may have stopped you in the past, it's time to look at two big obstacles that hold back most people, and how you can be among the few who know how to handle them. That's coming up in Chapter 4.

Website chapter bonus

At www.focusquick.com you'll find a video interview with personal effectiveness coach Carol Thompson on gaining positive patterns that can result in dramatic changes in your life.

4

CHAPTER FOUR

How to overcome the obstacles to focus

A crucial part of focusing on the vital 20% of what you do is to get rid of some of the 80% of activities that don't pay off very well. In this chapter you'll find out how to do that. There is also another obstacle, this one hidden, to doing the most useful things. Learning how to overcome it may be the single most important benefit you'll gain from reading this book. First, let's deal with the more obvious obstacle.

Getting rid of some of the less useful 80%

It sounds simple: stop doing the things that don't give you the greatest value so you can focus time and attention on the ones that do. But when you look more closely it becomes clear that many of the tasks in the 80% category support, and are necessary for, your high-value tasks.

Let's take a simple work-related example: filing. It's boring, tedious, and doesn't, in itself, bring any value to what you do. However, if you ignore it long enough, eventually your inability to find important documents will negatively affect some of the top-value things you do.

Another example: semi-social phone calls. Such calls may seem like a waste of time, yet they allow you to maintain contact with people whose cooperation may be vital to some of your top-value activities.

It's also easy to get caught up in doing research. Especially now that we have the internet, looking up a simple fact can easily lead to jumping to related interesting sites and suddenly an hour has gone. Obviously, the answer is not to skip doing the research, but rather to be aware of the potential distractions.

A final example: when writing, it's tempting to obsess about getting the perfect opening, writing and rewriting the first paragraph or the first page instead of getting on with the work and going back later to improve it. Here, too, the problem isn't that you're doing the wrong thing, but that you're doing the right thing in a way that is too time-consuming.

Each of these problems has a solution. Let's see what your options are.

Option one: eliminate or reduce

Usually, there are some activities that can be eliminated totally or on which we could spend less time. For most people this represents at least 10% to 15% of how they're spending their time. That may not sound like much but in an average workday this represents a gain of 45 minutes to an hour that can now be expended on high-value tasks. Consider for a moment how much you could achieve if you spent an extra hour a day on your number one goal.

Here are a few of the things, discussed in greater detail later, that most people could easily cut back on in their work:

- Taking in irrelevant information (see Chapter 11).
- Dealing inefficiently with paperwork (see Chapter 12).
- Spending too much time on email (see Chapter 13).
- Unproductive or unnecessary meetings (see Chapter 14).

Option two: delegate

The second step is to look at the remaining tasks and find which ones can be delegated to someone else. Remember, your goal is to spend the maximum amount of time on the things that bring you the most value. If you're doing your own filing, photocopying, errands, routine phone calls, etc., most likely you're wasting a lot of your time. Your options for delegating include:

- Hiring someone part time. Depending on the nature of the tasks, this could be a high school student or a university student, or a semi-retired person.
- Using virtual assistants. For many tasks your assistant doesn't need to be in your area – in fact, they may even be halfway around the world. Virtual assistants can handle secretarial, office, book-keeping, and computing services for you. To find these services just type "virtual assistant" into your search engine. When you find someone who performs to your satisfaction you can hire them on an ongoing basis.
- Using online freelancers. With services like elance.com you can specify a one-off project that you need, for

instance the design of a brochure. Freelancers from around the world will bid on it. You can see samples of their work first and read testimonials from others who have used them. You choose the person who you think will do the best job for the best price.

If you gain one hour a day from tasks you've eliminated and another hour a day by delegating, that's one full week per month you can now focus on your highest-value activities.

The secret of actually doing what you know you should

This brings us to the hidden obstacle that often stops people from applying what they know. Have you ever read a personal development book, thoughtfully underlined the important bits, and set out to implement its techniques and strategies . . . and found yourself a few weeks later back to doing things your old way? If so, then you've encountered this problem. You won't find this covered in most time management books because they are written by people who think in linear ways

Mona's experiment in delegating fails.

File, Rover, file!

and can't quite accept that logic seldom wins the day. They're not in tune with people who are right-brain, creative, and chaotic. Therefore, they also ignore what is the hidden obstacle to ever implementing their advice:

> Much of the time,
>
> doing what we should be doing
>
> is a lot less enjoyable
>
> than doing something else.

Making a phone call to try to sell someone a product or a new project isn't nearly as appealing as having a quick look at that book that might just have a chapter relevant to your business, or checking your email and the latest news.

If you look at the tasks related to your top-value activities, I bet you'll find that many of them are difficult, in some way unpleasant, or have risk of rejection associated with them.

If you look at your low-value activities, I bet you'll find they tend to be routine, unthreatening and maybe even enjoyable.

"low-value activities, tend to be routine, unthreatening and maybe even enjoyable. "

Now we've reached the real heart of the problem, the real reason why most people keep their 80/20 balance just the way it is, even if they know better.

Why do I call this a "secret" obstacle? Because so few people will admit to it!

Ask any of your friends or colleagues whether they have achieved their full potential. I doubt that many will say yes. Next ask them why this is. Some will blame outside forces: they didn't get the right education, they didn't meet the right people, the economic conditions weren't right, they received poor advice. Some will take responsibility and say they made errors of judgement or they got into the wrong line of business.

Only one in a thousand, if that, will say, "You know, it was because when I had to choose between doing the easy things and the difficult things, I generally took the easy path."

Many books and courses deliver pep talks to motivate you to do the difficult tasks. They get you revved up and tell you that you have to start taking risks. Some use the power of the crowd to notch up your energy. Some workshops have you break a board or walk across hot coals, or climb up a big pole. These can be great energy-boosters, but when you get back to the normal world the next morning, it all fades, and as much as you'd like to use your board-breaking skills in dealing with that difficult boss, it really isn't advisable.

What you need is a practical set of tools and techniques for making the difficult things easier and more enjoyable. It's human nature: when the formerly difficult tasks, the top-value tasks, start being as easy and enjoyable to accomplish as the low-value ones, you'll do more of them. When you do more of them, you create more value and get compensated for it.

Now you have the missing piece of the puzzle for the 80/20 rule: dumping unnecessary tasks, handing on the ones that can be delegated, and working more efficiently on the ones you do is only half the battle. The other half is making the

THE SECRET OF WALKING ON COALS

If you've wondered what allows people to fire-walk, the answer isn't mystical, it's simple physics. Here are some of the key factors: often the coals are covered with ash, which is a poor heat conductor; the coals are an uneven surface so the actual surface area of the feet touching the coals is very small; when the coal cools down it stops burning and no new heat is generated; and the walkers move across the coals briskly. The participants may get a mental boost by doing something they thought imposs-ible, but in fact anyone can do it.

top-value activities more enjoyable and easier to accomplish. Before we get into how you can do that, take a moment to go back to the list of your work activities you made in Chapter 2. By each item on your list, jot down a number from one to ten, with one signifying an activity that you hate to do and ten signifying one you really enjoy doing. (Go on, do it now, I'll wait . . .)

Did the activities you spend most time on, but that don't produce the most value, get higher scores than the three most valuable ones? If so, then applying the techniques in the rest of this chapter are likely to produce a real breakthrough in your productivity.

If not, then your challenge may not be that you don't enjoy the top three, but that you have let the demands of other people, or "urgent but not important" tasks dominate your time. In that case, still read the rest of this chapter but you may find that your bigger breakthrough comes via the strat-egies covered later in the book.

Chunking down to get started

One thing that can make a task seem daunting and unpleasant is its sheer size. In that case, the secret is to break it down into easy-to-do small chunks. Keep making the chunks smaller and smaller until the task is so easy to achieve that you have no problem facing it. For example, let's say you have to make a phone call firing your current website developer. You know it's going to be unpleasant, so you don't do it. But you can't get on to hiring a new person until the old one is gone, so this is delaying the revamping of your website. In turn, that's limiting the amount of revenue the site is generating. This "for the want of a nail, a kingdom was lost" phenomenon is very common. First, check whether this task can be eliminated – no. Second, can it be delegated? Possibly, but if not, then you can chunk the phone call down into these steps:

- Find and write down the person's phone number.

- Jot down what you want to say and how you want to say it.

- Prepare for the worst eventuality. In this case, that might be a very emotional or hostile reaction, and you could be prepared to say something like, "I'm sorry that this is upsetting you so much, and I will send you a written statement to confirm that our arrangement will not be continuing." If it sounds like it may turn into a legal problem, tell the other person that the rest of the matter will be handled by your lawyer. In most cases, the worst will not happen.

- Now think about the outcome, not the task. How relieved will you feel once you've finished this call? How good will it be not to be dreading it anymore? Use this positive anticipation to propel you to doing the task.

> "He has the deed half done who has made a beginning."
> *Horace. Roman Poet, 65BC–8BC*

Some people feel a bit silly about breaking a task down into micro-tasks, but it's a great way to prime the pump. For instance, if you have resolved to go to the gym three times a week and find yourself resisting it, commit to just stepping outside your front door with your gym bag in hand. Tell yourself that if you want to turn back once you've done that, you can. In fact, once you find yourself outside with the bag in hand it's highly likely that you'll carry on.

Similarly, if you need to write a report, commit only to writing the first sentence. Most likely you'll keep going.

Try it now. Choose one task that relates to one of your goals and that you have been avoiding. Break it down into three or more chunks:

The task:_____

Chunk 1:_____

Chunk 2:_____

Chunk 3:_____

Chunk 4:_____

Chunk 5:_____

Chunk 6:_____

How do you feel about doing only Chunk 1 today? If it's practical, you could do it right now and get the feeling of satisfaction of knowing you've started. If you feel like going on, do so; otherwise, put Chunk 2 on your "to do" list for tomorrow and keep going, day by day, until you've achieved it.

Who says you have to start at the beginning?

In many cases you don't need to start at the beginning. When I coach people who have writer's block, for instance, I advise them to get a pack of index cards and throughout the day jot down any ideas that pop into their minds. This can just as easily apply to writing a business plan, developing an invention, or any other big goal. Keep all the cards and review them once a week or so and see both how they fit together and what additional ideas they prompt. Then decide on one piece of the greater work that you can do now. If you're writing a novel, you might have in mind the big showdown scene that will occur somewhere toward the end. There's no reason why you can't write that scene first and then work your way toward it. If you are coming up with a new product and you have an idea for the packaging, go ahead and work on that even before you've finished the product itself. If you start with the bits that excite you the most right now, you create momentum for the rest.

Take a minute to think about one of your goals. What parts of it are the most appealing, whether or not they relate to the logical beginning? What parts excite you enough to get started on today or tomorrow?

CAPTURING YOUR IDEAS

If you don't capture your ideas the moment they occur, most likely you will forget them. You can carry a pen and notebook or index cards, a small digital tape recorder, or you can phone yourself and leave the idea on your voice mail. Harvest the ideas frequently to decide which ones to implement.

Create a flow

You may be familiar with the concept of "flow" as written about extensively by Professor Mihaly Csikszentmihalyi (pronounced "chick-sent-me-high"). It's that state in which you are so involved with whatever you are doing that you lose all track of time. Often it's an exhilarating experience in which it seems like you are just a medium for whatever you are doing – a state of intense yet effortless focus. The question is, how can you induce such a state rather than waiting and hoping for it to occur spontaneously? Here are three keys:

1. **Pick a task that is at or just above your level of ability**. If it's too hard or too easy, you won't enter flow. So if you want to write something, break it down into chunks you can handle. One might be writing a rough outline. Another might be jotting down key points in a list or making a mind map. Write down one task like this that relates to one of your goals:

   _____

2. **Make sure that the task includes immediate feedback**, so that you know as you go along whether or not you are doing well. For instance, you can start by setting yourself a goal of writing a certain number of words, or getting a specific needed piece of information during your first one hour work session. Generally, you need to feel positive at the early stages, and eventually the task may so absorb you that you stop thinking about how you're doing it, or how well. Write down what measure will give you this feedback for the task you jotted down above:

   _____

3. **Create an atmosphere in which you have as few distractions as possible**. Again, later in the process you may

be so involved that you don't even notice things like a phone ringing, but it helps if you can start off in an environment that makes it easy to concentrate. This also includes setting aside a period of time when you won't feel you really should be doing something else. Write down when and where you will work without distraction on the task you chose above:

_____

Schedule some time during which you want to tackle a task that supports your highest-value goal and create all of the conditions described above. Go into the process with the idea that if flow occurs, that will be great, and if it doesn't, you'll still get a lot done (that mentality makes it less likely that you'll distract yourself by asking "Am I in flow yet?").

Using odd chunks of time

The strategy of chunking applies to time as well. It's possible to carve out some odd periods of time in which we can get a lot done, but it requires some new strategies. Here are three suggestions:

1. Into your TV guide put a sticky note that reads, "7.30–8.30pm The Goal Hour, starring myself". Then replace an hour, or half-hour, of TV watching with a working session. A year from now, what would you regret more: not having seen a season of *The X Factor*, or not having made progress toward your most cherished goal?

2. On your shopping list, add "20 Minutes of Goal Work". When you go out to shop, take 20 minutes beforehand or afterward to go to a nearby coffee shop and work on your project.

3. The next time your children or partner want you to go to a movie that you're not really keen to see, go to the cinema with them, let them go in, and go to a nearby coffee shop and work on your goal until it's time for them to come out, then take them for an ice cream and let them tell you all about the film.

CREATING FLOW IN A GROUP

Csikszentmihalyi suggsts ways that a group can encourage flow, including: having a diverse group; no tables, so people will stand and move; lots of ways to record ideas, including charts and graphs; and a playful atmosphere.

Invent your own strategies for overcoming the obstacle

All of the strategies in this chapter are about making it easier and more enjoyable to do the tasks that you might otherwise avoid. There are many others, including:

- do them while listening to music you enjoy
- do them together with someone you like
- reward yourself with some kind of treat whenever you finish a task
- bet someone else that you can do the tasks, and make sure that losing the bet would hurt.

You probably have a good idea of what motivates you the most. Some people respond better to rewards (getting a promotion), some to punishment (the threat of losing a job). What works best for you? Jot down three techniques or strategies that you will use to make it easier to achieve tasks you might otherwise avoid – these can be ones from this chapter, or ones you make up yourself:

1. _____

2. _____

3. _____

This time when you move toward your goals, you know the secret: that you have to make space to focus on the most important 20%, and you have to make difficult tasks as enjoyable as the easy ones. In the next chapter you'll find out how to use another key strategy: focusing on what already works.

Website chapter bonus

At www.focusquick.com you'll find a video interview with actor, improviser and creativity coach Roddy Maude-Roxby on transforming tedious tasks into enjoyable ones.

5

How to focus on what already works

Do you know that in the process of trying to achieve success, most people focus on the opposite of what they should be doing? It's true, and probably this is a mistake you have made in the past as well. Once you turn this around, your success will accelerate dramatically.

The mistaken strategy is to focus on your weaknesses instead of your strengths. Let's look at some examples of hugely successful people and brands to see what they do. Donald Trump and Richard Branson are both super self-promoters. They figure out how to make a news event out of every new venture, and usually it's not their own money that is financing the bulk of the projects. They are pro-motable brand names, and that's what they focus on. They have other people to handle the nitty-gritty aspects of their business.

It's the same with product brands. The key trait of all Apple products is their great design. They don't try to be the cheapest or the most popular. Wal-Mart, on the other hand, has made itself the most successful retail business in the world by being the cheapest and the biggest.

Contrast this focus with the attitudes of most people. They identify their weaknesses and focus on trying to fix those. While they're busy becoming passable at what they don't do well, they're not giving their time to the things at which they excel. It's a prescription for mediocrity.

When you do the 80/20 analysis, usually you find that the 20% that will give you the most value is something you already do, but you're just not doing enough of it. Similarly, when looking for strategies that will help you succeed, it makes sense to look at what is already working for you and simply do it more often or apply it to more challenges in your life. In this chapter you'll discover what your strengths are, and learn how to apply them for maximum impact.

> "Everyone should carefully observe which way his heart draws him, and then choose that way with all his strength."
> *Hasidic saying*

The point is so important that it bears repeating: if you want to join the top 5% of achievers in any field, you will have to do more of what you do well, and worry less about becoming good at what you don't do well. It's perfectly logical, isn't it? If you already do something well and then put even more energy into it, you're going to do it *extremely* well. It will put you far ahead of most others doing that thing. On the other hand, if there's something you don't do well at all, and you put effort into getting better at it, the odds are that with a lot of work you'll become mediocre. Of course you can't just ignore the necessary things you don't do well, but you can put your energy into finding people who do those things better than you ever could, and delegate or outsource those things to them. For example, check which of these give you a shiver of excitement and which give you a shiver of fear:

- Sales.
- Accounting.
- Public speaking.
- Web design.
- Brainstorming sessions.
- Networking.
- Marketing.
- Meetings.

There's nothing inherently evil or awful about any of these, except accounting. Just kidding. It strikes terror into my heart, but there are people who live for it, whereas I quite enjoy public speaking and some accountants would rather throw themselves under a bus than get up to speak in front of a group. It's not even only about what you enjoy. I'd like to learn how to do web design myself, but I realise that it wouldn't be a good use of my time and I'd probably never do it as well as the professionals, so I delegate it. With online services like the ones I've already mentioned, such as elance.com, it's easier than ever to find people to do the things you can't or don't want to do.

What are your strengths?

I bet if I asked you what your greatest weaknesses are you'd be able to reel them off without much effort. Most people, however, are not able to identify their strengths as easily, even though knowing that is essential. So let's take an inventory of your strengths. Jot down the first answer that comes to mind for the following questions:

1. What is your greatest strength when it comes to having new ideas?

   _____

2. What is your greatest strength when it comes to expressing yourself?

   _____

3. What is your greatest strength when it comes to dealing with other people?

   _____

4. What is your greatest strength when it comes to getting things done?

   _____

Of course there are certain things that you want to do and that relate to your strengths, but you don't always do them as effectively as you could. In that case, one good way to find out how to do them better is to look at the times when you *do* perform them well.

When do you do the right thing?

I once coached a writer who said she was "always" late for meetings. They were vital to her work and they weren't unpleasant, so she wasn't trying to avoid them, but she seldom got to them on time. Naturally this didn't endear her to editors, agents, or others who had to wait for her to show up.

A closer examination showed that there was an important exception: the writer never missed a plane. Obviously she had a different pattern when she had a plane to catch. The question was, what did she already do differently at those times, that she could now also start to do in other situations when she's supposed to be somewhere by a particular time?

Her answer was that when she was flying somewhere she did all of her packing and preparation the previous day. We then looked at how she could do a mini-version of that kind of advance preparation to get ready for other obligations, and it made a huge difference.

Here are some questions along these lines that might be helpful for you:

- If you generally procrastinate, what DON'T you procrastinate about?

- If you generally don't finish projects that you start, but once in a while you do, what is different about those?

- If you generally don't start your workday by doing the most important thing, but some days you do, what's different about those days?

In the exceptions to unproductive patterns, you will find clues to change. Quite often, the problem contains the seeds of its own solution.

You can give this approach a try right now.

First jot down one thing you generally don't handle as well as you'd like to:

_____

Now think of at least one time when you did handle it well:

_____

What was different about the time you did it well?

_____

How can you apply this the next time you have to do the same task?

Notice when things are going right

An even better way to learn to make a habit of using your most effective traits and behaviours is to notice them as they are happening. Most of us don't do this – we notice when things are going badly, but when they're going well we take it for granted. From now on, spend a few minutes at the end of each day reviewing what happened and take note of what worked well for you and why. For instance, if you managed to clear up your backlog of email, why was this easy to do today? Maybe you set yourself a deadline of 30 minutes for working through all of them, and the ticking clock kept you from getting distracted by interesting but not really relevant emails, or maybe you figured out a new way to use a system of folders to sort the emails more effectively.

YOUR NIGHTLY REVIEW

A good way to remember to do a review of your day and what you can learn from what went right is to link it to something you do every night, like brushing your teeth. Keep a pen and paper nearby so you can jot down your insights.

Now take another couple of minutes to consider how you could apply these techniques that work to any other challenges you're facing at the moment. Would it make sense to set a similar deadline for writing a rough first draft of that report you've been meaning to do? Could you use a version of your new email folders system to bring more order to your paperwork?

Even better is to jot down all the things that work well so that every time in the future that you face a difficult task you can review your list and find the proven methods that will help you the most in tackling the new challenge. The best thing about this approach is that you are learning from yourself, knowing that these are strategies that have already proved themselves.

Learn from Pavlov and his drooling dogs

Do you remember reading or hearing about Pavlov's dogs? The Russian scientist rang a bell whenever he fed the dogs. The sight of the food made the dogs drool. After a while, all he had to do to get them to drool was to ring the bell. They associated the sound with the food so closely that their bodies reacted as though the food were there. You may be wondering how this is relevant, since you probably have no desire to make dogs drool unnecessarily. Well, this same phenomenon of "classical conditioning" is one you can use to your advantage.

There are times when you're performing at the top of your game, but for most of us those physical and mental states come and go, and they feel out of our control. Wouldn't it be great if you could trigger those states whenever you wanted to? You can, by using the same principle that Pavlov utilised. When you realise you are in a particularly productive state of mind, link it to a sound (for instance, a particular song that you play on your stereo – be sure to pick something you don't play too often) or

a smell (for example, from a bottle of peppermint oil, or even an aftershave or perfume you don't normally use). When you have done this a few times, the state of mind and the other element will be linked to the degree that when you expose yourself to the sound or smell the positive state will also appear. We'll look at a variation of this approach in the next chapter, where you'll learn how to use the Alter Ego strategy.

When and where do you get your best ideas?

A survey conducted by BT and *Management Today* magazine revealed that two-thirds of the managers responding have their best ideas outside of work. When and where do you have your best ideas? Typical answers are:

- In the shower.
- In the bath.
- While shaving.
- Driving to work.
- On the train or the Underground.

- While playing golf.
- While walking or jogging.
- In bed, right after waking up.
- In bed, right before falling asleep.
- During the adverts when watching TV.
- At the gym.

Circle any of the above that apply to you and if you have different answers jot them down here:

_____

_____

_____

As we've already noted elsewhere, it's vital that you capture any great ideas before you're distracted and they vanish. Put pads of paper and pens anywhere in the house where you're likely to have ideas: in the bathroom, by your bed, by the sofa in the living room, in the kitchen. If you come up with insights in places where it's impractical to write things down, such as while jogging or working out, consider taking along a little tape recorder or an MP3 player that can be adapted to record as well.

"_it's vital that you capture any great ideas before you're distracted_**"**

How to harness the power of daydreams

Unfortunately, we're told when we're growing up that daydreams are a foolish waste of time, yet that's exactly what you're doing when you're in the shower, or on a walk, or on the treadmill at the gym and suddenly an idea pops into your mind. The information is coming from your subconscious mind, which is fed by a multitude of your conscious activities. There's no way to force this kind of productive daydreaming, but there are some ways to invite it to occur more frequently. If you'd like to have it happen more often:

- Make more time for the kinds of activities during which you tend to have ideas (e.g., take longer baths).

- When ideas come up, don't judge them right away. A negative thought will quickly kill a new idea. Even if your first impulse is that the idea is impractical or irrelevant, stay with it. It may lead to another idea that works.

- Never try to force ideas but do play around with them. For instance, if you want to figure out how to give a powerful presentation, let your thoughts wander back to good and bad presentations you've seen and notice what pops into your mind. If they come up, entertain "crazy" ideas (what kind of presentation would Homer Simpson give . . .).

A hidden source of ideas: your night dreams

It has long been known that many great writers were inspired by their dreams, including Robert Louis Stevenson for *Dr. Jekyll and Mr. Hyde*. Paul McCartney dreamed the tune for the song *Yesterday*. Madame C. J. Walker had a dream in which she was shown how to mix a hair-care product that made her America's first female self-made millionaire. If you never remember or write down your dreams, you may be missing out on a great source of information.

Research suggests you can even use dreams to solve specific problems. A study reported in the *Journal of Sleep Research* (December, 2004) got 470 people to write down their dreams and rate them in terms of their intensity, emotions, and

TRY STRUCTURED DAYDREAMING

If you want to use daydreaming to solve a problem, pick a word at random from a magazine and try to figure out how that word might relate to a solution, For example, if you want to convince your boss about the value of a new idea, and the word you hit upon is "doctor," your thoughts might lead you to the notion that a doctor is a respected authority figure, and maybe you need an expert's endorsement of your idea.

impact. The participants were asked to also recall various events that took place up to a week before. Then independent judges evaluated the dreams to see whether they contained possible solutions for problems arising from those events. Their conclusion: dreams do offer insights and solutions in the week after the problem comes up. The solutions can appear in dreams as quickly as the night after the problem first arises, but also six to seven days later.

You can make it more likely that this will happen if you focus on the problem shortly before you go to sleep. Don't do it in the form of worrying, but rather as a question to which you expect an answer. Then go to sleep. The next morning jot down any dreams you remember. Don't analyse yet, just write down everything you can remember. If the dream wakes you up, record it then (you might forget by morning). The next day, sit down in a quiet place and look over what you've written. Dreams are metaphors, so the solution to your problem may appear as some kind of symbol. Let your mind flow free to come up with ideas of what the dream may be trying to tell you.

You now have a much better idea of the strengths that are going to be the key to propelling you to the success you desire. When you do what you know is the right thing to do, you have immense power. However, most people find that power sapped by procrastination. In the next chapter, you will learn how to overcome that negative habit once and for all.

Website chapter bonus

At www.focusquick.com you will find a downloadable MP3 guided visualisation that helps you identify one of your key strengths and lets you imagine how you could use it to help you solve a challenge or problem you're facing at the moment.

6

How to (finally) beat procrastination

Procrastination is the natural enemy of focus. When we procrastinate, we do everything other than the things that we know we should be doing. It is the biggest problem that almost everyone has with moving toward their goals so it deserves a whole chapter by itself. As you'll see, there are a variety of approaches you can take to overcome procrastination. Once you've found the one that works best for you, you'll have the edge over almost all your competitors.

First: are you sure you have a problem?

Before we start looking at the cures, let's make sure you actually have the disease. If you put things off until what seems like the last minute, but then you get them done, and done well every time, you're not procrastinating. You're just choosing to spend your time on other things until it's really time to work on a particular project, and then you do it. You've learned how to judge accurately how long something is going to take and you don't like to start early. If the only thing bothering you is that someone else has characterised this as procrastination, ignore them and keep on doing what you're doing, because it's working.

SHAKESPEARE ON TIME

"Better three hours too soon than one minute too late."
The Merry Wives of Windsor

"I wasted time, and now doth time waste me."
King Richard II

If, on the other hand, you miss deadlines or find that leaving things until the last minute causes you stress, you are a procrastinator and using the techniques in this chapter will help you.

The temptations of procrastination

To understand the dynamics of procrastination, let's look at how temptation works. Generally you have a choice between two or more things. Sometimes it's a simple "yes or no" choice: should you have this piece of chocolate cake or not? Sometimes it's a choice between activities: will you stay in and watch TV or will you go to the gym to exercise? What determines your choice?

When Isaac Newton set out his laws of motion, he also unwittingly formulated some of laws of human behaviour. Here's how the first one is often stated:

> An object at rest tends to stay at rest and an object in motion tends to stay in motion with the same speed and in the same direction unless acted upon by an unbalanced force.

In human terms, a body at rest on a sofa tends to stay at rest. And a body in motion in a certain direction (e.g., having a nice dinner) will tend to continue in that direction (eating a big piece of chocolate cake for dessert).

So, in order to change direction, we have to make some effort. But why is this so hard when we are aware of the benefits of, for example, eating healthy food, exercising, or working on tasks in a measured way rather than putting them off until the last minute?

One reason is that the attractiveness of the "bad" option is very strong in the here and now. The attractiveness of the "good" option (or the punishment for ignoring it) tends to be weak in the here and now, and strong only in the long term. Here's the key fact: generally, the "good" option pays off in the long run. The "bad" option pays off immediately. Therefore, the "bad" option is stronger in the moment.

For example, if I choose to spend the next couple of hours surfing the web, that's fun right now. Maybe I really should be working on a report that's due in two weeks, but if I don't do that, there is no immediate punishment or drawback. The punishment arrives in a week, when I realise I'm now hopelessly behind, or in two weeks, when I miss the deadline and my client gets angry with me.

Here's the other crucial difference: the short-term option often strongly engages our senses and emotions, whereas the long-term option – because it is not present right now – only engages our intellect.

In the battle between emotion and intellect, which do you think wins most of the time? Hint: take a look around at our world, at the wars, the spoiling of the environment, the personal debt level of the average person – the answer is all too clear.

The chocolate cake looks great, smells good, feels creamy on our tongue, and tastes wonderful! The idea of losing weight ... er, well, it's a nice idea ... and at times, such as when we are overcome with guilt, it does have an impact. Unfortunately, this usually happens only after we overindulge.

Here is the key that will allow you to make the better choice every time: the secret of choosing the "good" option is to make it as vivid, emotional, and compelling in the moment as the "bad" option.

How do you do this? By using your imagination to see, hear, taste, smell, and feel the "good" choice even more strongly than the "bad" choice.

Close your eyes and start to visualize the **outcome** of the "good" choice. This is important: don't visualise yourself doing the task, visualise the end result or a step along the way.

What will you **see** when you've done this? For example, what will you see when your business, for which you are just starting to write the business plan, is successful? If the business is a store you can visualise the premises thronged with enthusiastic customers.

What will you **hear**? Maybe you can imagine the customers complimenting you on the goods you are selling, or phoning their friends to tell them about your business.

What will you **feel**? This may be the most important of all – perhaps you will feel proud, happy, excited, joyful.

Sometimes **smell** comes into it as well. You might imagine yourself smelling the fresh flowers you have set up on the counter of your store.

> If you have trouble getting into a visualisation of the result you want, start by remembering a similar time when you achieved something that gave you great satisfaction. Remember with all your senses what that was like, and then transfer these characteristics to the outcome of your current goal.

Even **taste** can be a factor. Maybe you imagine a dinner held to celebrate the opening of your business and someone toasts you and you drink a glass of champagne.

The more vivid and exciting you can make this, the more energy you will free up for getting started.

As with every exercise in this book, play around until you find the form that works best for you. For instance, some people might find it too scary to think ahead as far as the opening of their business; they might consider it more compelling to imagine just getting the loan they need in order to rent premises, or even just imagining the banker giving them compliments on their finished business plan.

When you've visualised whatever is most motivating for you, stay in that state of excitement after you open your eyes, and suddenly watching TV or surfing the internet will seem pretty boring by comparison. Launch into the task while the feeling is still fresh.

Add more focus with the power of an anchor

For the visualisation technique to work you have to do it. For you to do it you have to pause instead of just giving in to the path of least resistance. It's a bit like remembering to count to ten when you're angry instead of immediately flying off the handle. So that you don't have to take the time to do this every time you are tempted, it's useful to "anchor" the desired state in a way that will make it easier for you to make the choice that is best for you. You've already read about this method and how it's derived from the work of Pavlov and his dogs. Now let's see how you can use it in situations where you want to avoid procrastinating:

- Choose a state that represents your positive feelings about the outcome of whatever you tend to procrastinate about. If you tend to put off exercising, use the state of fantastic healthful energy that comes from exercising. If you tend to put off working on a long-term project, use the state of the joy of having finished the project. If you tend to put off doing administrative tasks, use the state of relief and peace of mind that comes when they are out of the way.

- Stand up, close your eyes and, using your memory or your imagination, create as vivid a representation of that positive state as you can. Include what you see, hear, feel, and maybe taste and smell when you experience that state.

- Keep "turning up the volume" of these feelings until they feel really strong.

- When you attain a peak, make a gesture like squeezing together your thumb and forefinger. Hold it for a second, then release. This becomes your anchor, the signal that you will experience this state.

- Repeat the process a few times, ideally spread out over a day or two.

- To check how strong the association is, "drop the anchor" – that is, make the gesture and monitor your feelings. If the feeling isn't strong yet, keep practising.

The next time you are tempted to procrastinate, make the appropriate gesture and you will find it easier to opt for the activity that will lead to your desired outcome.

Your reasons for resistance and how to overcome them

There may also be deeper reasons for your resistance to doing a particular task. If so, it will help you to identify those reasons or beliefs and challenge them. Here are the most common kinds of resistance and how to overcome them.

Because the conditions aren't right

Make a list of all the conditions you believe you need. Will these ever exist? If not, break your project down into small chunks and ask yourself whether the conditions are adequate for you to achieve the first small chunk. The answer probably will be yes, so do that chunk and then move on to the next one. If you still have trouble, make the chunks smaller and smaller.

Because I work best in a crisis

If you're a crisis junkie, consider giving yourself that adrenaline jolt some other way: bungee jumping, maybe? Seriously, try interspersing work sessions with a high-action computer game or hard exercise.

Because I don't want to and you can't make me!

Practise saying no to things you don't want to do. If there's any way to make the unwanted work go away, do it early on (by delegating, for example). If not, make an assessment of how doing the task will benefit you, and keep those benefits in mind.

Because I insist on perfection

Give yourself permission to do it imperfectly. Practise doing some small things imperfectly and notice what happens (or what doesn't happen). Work on toning down your harsh inner critic.

Because it drives somebody else crazy, ha ha!

If your procrastination is a way of rebelling against those who ask you do to things, consider whether there are more straightforward ways of expressing your anger or resentment or establishing a feeling of control. Often the best way to do this is not to take on the work in the first place, if possible.

Because it doesn't feel good

It doesn't have to feel good, it just has to get done. But it's easier if you combine it with something that does feel good (e.g., listening to music while sorting through receipts for your tax statement), or reward yourself when the task is done.

What's your reason?

Which of the above do you think is closest to your reasons for procrastinating?

_____

HOW TO (FINALLY) BEAT PROCRASTINATION

What will you do differently the next time you want to overcome your procrastination?

_____

If you're still not sure . . .

There may be times when you're not sure why you're procrastinating, and getting more clarity about it could be what helps you to overcome this block. At those times it's helpful to ask yourself some questions. The following sentence completion technique is great for this because it brings to the surface things that may have been lodged in your subconscious mind. Once the facts are out you can deal with them with one of the techniques we've already covered. If there's something you're procrastinating about at the moment, try doing the sentence completion exercise overleaf; if not, keep it handy for the next time procrastination is an issue.

Taking the first step

The first step is often the hardest. Rather than tackle what seems to be a daunting task, it's easier to put it off and do something else. In an earlier chapter you learned about the technique of chunking down a large task into small steps. The smaller the chunk, the easier it is to accomplish and the sooner you have the feeling that you're on the way to reaching your goal.

❝The smaller the chunk, the easier it is to accomplish❞

The reason this works has been uncovered by the Procrastination Research Group run by Prof. Timothy Pychyl

PROCRASTINATION SENTENCE COMPLETION

Write down the first thoughts that come to mind to complete each statement. The task I am procrastinating about is:

_____

1. One thing that's important to remember about this task is

_____

2. One person who could help me with this task is

_____

3. A similar task I've done successfully was

_____

4. One thing nobody knows about this task is

_____

5. A good symbol for this task is

_____

6. I'll know this task has been accomplished successfully when

_____

7. A good song title for this problem/challenge would be

_____

8. One personal quality that could really help me with doing this task is

_____

9. If I had a magic wand to use to change one aspect of this task, I'd change

_____

Len takes his first small step towards fitness.

at Ottawa's Carleton University. His studies reveal that there seem to be two ways people function: some are action-oriented, and they switch easily from task to task; others are state-oriented, and they are more likely to procrastinate and suffer more from uncertainty, frustration, boredom and guilt. If you're state-oriented, Pychyl suggests acknowledging that you don't feel like doing the task, but promise yourself you'll do it for ten minutes. By the time you get to the end of that period, most likely your state will have shifted and you'll be able to continue.

You can also extend the small chunks strategy by identifying a set of milestones that you will reach along the way to your goal. Research shows how powerful this can be: a 2001 study by Dan Ariely at the MIT Sloan School of Management and Klaus Wertenbroch at Insead gave one group a large task with only an end deadline, another group weekly deadlines leading toward the completion of the task. The group who had only one deadline were, on average, 12 days late. The ones who had weekly deadlines were, on average, only half a day late.

MAKE IT VISUAL

For larger projects you can draw a thermometer and label the intervals with the tasks you need to accomplish and your target dates. Colour in the segments of the thermometer as you complete each task. Keep it where you (and, ideally, others) can see it every day.

Procrastination and your "to do" list

Handling the "to do" list is probably the area in which the most people experience procrastination. As well as using the methods we've already covered, it might be helpful to identify your type. There are three basic ones:

1. **The Puritans:** do the hardest things first, then enjoy doing the rest. These people eat their Brussels sprouts first.

2. **The Hedonists:** do one or two easy things first, gradually glide into doing the more difficult things. These people eat their pudding first.

3. **The Gamblers:** write each task on an index card, and with eyes shut, shuffle them. Then do them in the order they come up (no fair re-shuffling!). This panders to the gambler's love of the unpredictable.

Which one is best? Whichever one works for you. Try them all, then follow the one that allows you to get the most important things done during the course of your day.

You now have an impressive set of strategies you can use to defeat procrastination and to focus on what will speed you toward success. In Part 3 you will discover a set of innovative focus tools that make this journey even easier and faster.

Website chapter bonus

At www.focusquick.com you will find a downloadable "kick start" brief guided visualisation to listen to when you need a boost to concentrate your energy on a task you've been avoiding.

Part

3

Your focus tools

7

How to use the Alter Ego strategy

In the previous chapter you found out how you can use your strengths to help you focus on the important task at hand. Different tasks require different states of mind. Extreme example: sorting out your tax receipts vs. coming up with a name for a new product. The good news is that whether you know it or not, you already have these states within you. In this chapter you'll find out how you can choose your state of mind and use this power to transform your use of time. The result will be that you will approach all tasks with maximum focus and effectiveness.

You have many personalities

Research has shown that the idea that a person has a stable, unchangeable personality that extends across all situations is an illusion. We act differently in different situations. The same person may be generous in some situations and stingy in others; gentle at times and aggressive at others, and so on.

❝We act differently in different situations. ❞

Sometimes how we act depends on the people we're with. Even as adults, for example, many people tend to revert to acting in a rather childlike way or to being on their best behaviour when they're with their parents.

TWO VIEWS OF CONSISTENCY

"Consistency requires you to be as ignorant today as you were a year ago."
Bernard Berenson, Art Historian (1865–1959)

"Consistency is the last refuge of the unimaginative."
Oscar Wilde, Writer and Wit (1854–1900)

Sometimes how we act depends on the level of stress we are experiencing. Possibly you've been with a usually gentle and nice person who flew into a rage when they were pushed just that little bit too far. They may later say, "I'm sorry, I wasn't myself," but really they were themselves, just a different and perhaps usually rare version of themselves.

There's nothing wrong with this inconsistency; in fact, it makes sense that we tailor our behaviour to the situation. But most people are not aware that they have a choice about how to respond, and that the range of choices they have represents a huge potential asset. Instead, people tend to ascribe their moods, attitudes, and even their behaviours to outside factors, with statements like these:

"He makes me so mad."

"When she looks at me that way, I just can't say no."

"When my to do list gets too long, I can't help going into a panic."

You do have a choice

The Alter Ego strategy relates to deciding which of your many personalities would be most helpful in a given situation, and putting that one in charge. I call these personalities your Alter Egos. By putting the right one in charge, you will find that you get things done more effectively, efficiently, and with less stress, even with enjoyment.

You can do this when you react to a situation as well as when you are planning to do a particular task. First, if you tend to respond to certain situations in a non-constructive way, you can stop that response and substitute another one. One example of this is the "counting to ten" rule when you're getting angry. It gives you time to consider whether your mounting anger is really going to help the situation, and to respond differently. Even though the "hothead you" may want to be in charge, you can choose to put the "assertive but calm you" in control instead.

It works just as well when you are getting ready to handle a task. Let's say you have to clean out the garage but you really don't feel like it. You'd much prefer to lounge around and read the magazines that came in the post this morning. You could procrastinate and not clean the garage, or you could force yourself to do it, but still think about the fact that it would be nice to be lounging and reading. If you do the latter, cleaning the garage will probably take you a long time, be haphazard, and certainly be no fun.

Here's how you could apply the Alter Ego technique to this situation.

First, pretend for a moment that you were going to hire someone to do the job for you. What kind of attributes and attitudes would you like this person to have? These might include being focused, not getting distracted, being rational (not sentimental) about what to throw away, being efficient, moving quickly and with purpose.

Second, remember a time when you exhibited all or most of these qualities yourself. It need not have anything to do with the task at hand. It may be that you need to combine memories (for example, the time you were totally focused, and the time you were rational about what needed to be done might be two different events).

Third, stand up and use your memories to get into that state now. It helps to close your eyes and take a few minutes to get into this fully. Remember what you **see** when you feel this way, what you **hear** (for example, what you say to yourself or what others say to you), and **how it feels** inside to be this way. If you don't have strong memories to draw upon, create the feelings using your imagination. It can be helpful to give this version of yourself a playful name.

Now put this Alter Ego in charge and do whatever you need to do. If you find yourself snapping out of it, stop and quickly get back into the desired state. For instance, if you come across some old magazines in the garage and start to peruse them, stop, re-focus, and get back to work.

A gallery of Alter Egos

Here are a few Alter Egos you might find useful.

Miss Moneypenny: Rational, efficient, conservative. Good person to put in charge when preparing your taxes, deciding about purchases, etc.

Attila: Strong, constantly aware of the goal, unyielding. Good person to put in charge when you've previously let others ride roughshod over your interests or needs, or when you've let yourself get too distracted from the task at hand.

Albert: Thinks out of the box, not afraid of failure or ridicule. Good person to put in charge when you need to be creative. A good choice for when you're brainstorming.

Big Kid: Playful, adventurous, open-minded. Good person to put in charge when you find yourself taking things too seriously.

Mightyman/Mightywoman: Strong, self-assured, capable. Good person to put in charge when confidence is necessary, such as making presentations, making a phone call you're not sure about, etc.

Sister Harmonia: Gentle, conciliatory, interested in finding the win-win situation for everybody concerned. Good person to put in charge when negotiating with reasonable people.

MORE ALTER EGOS

If you have trouble making up your own Alter Egos, watch a morning of cartoons and pick out the characters that work best for the moods you might want. If a moment calls for playful cheerfulness, SpongeBob Squarepants might just come in handy.

These are some of the Alter Egos I find useful; you may find it more helpful to come up with your own. Also, it may be necessary to change personalities in the middle of a situation – for example, if Sister Harmonia isn't getting anywhere in a negotiation, at some point Attila may have to take over! But I hope you can see how things can go wrong when we unthinkingly let the wrong person take charge. You really don't want Big Kid doing your tax returns, or Attila in charge of a first meeting with a possible client.

From now on you can choose which of your many personalities to put in charge. Here's a quick summary of the process:

1. Analyse the task at hand. What qualities are required in order to handle it?

2. Use your memories and/or your imagination to create or recreate a personality who has those qualities, and get into the desired state. Give this Alter Ego a name.

3. Put this Alter Ego in charge until the task is done, or until you reach a point at which a different one is called for.

4. Complete the task, then consciously step out of that personality into either your more typical self, or into another Alter Ego that fits whatever you wish to do next.

Try out an Alter Ego

Now it's time for you to plan how this technique will work for you. Below, write three types of tasks that you feel you could handle more effectively than you do now. Examples might include processing email, catching up with administrative backlog, making calls to potential clients, and getting started on a new project.

Task 1: _____

Task 2: _____

Task 3: _____

Give a name to the Alter Ego that tends to handle each task for you now. For example, sometimes I find that I let the Big Kid check my email – which means that I follow all the interesting links, get distracted reading the news, etc. and an hour later I'm still not finished actually processing my email.

AE who usually handles task 1: _____

AE who usually handles task 2: _____

AE who usually handles task 3: _____

In the three blanks below, give a name to the Alter Ego who you think might do a better job of handling that task. In my case, probably Attila would be more appropriate, because he's ruthless about zapping unimportant emails.

Better AE for task 1: _____

Better AE for task 2: _____

Better AE for task 3: _____

Finally, in the blanks below jot down how you think this preferred Alter Ego would handle the task. If it helps, close your eyes for a moment and get into character. In my example,

Attila would immediately delete the junk mail, then he'd briskly put the other emails into folders to be handled at appropriate times. Before actually answering any, I might want to switch to a different Alter Ego, as Attila tends to be pretty brusque.

How new AE would handle task 1: _____

_____

_____

How new AE would handle task 2: _____

_____

_____

How new AE would handle task 3: _____

_____

_____

Hire The Consultant in the mirror

An Alter Ego that can be useful in a variety of situations is The Consultant. You can get a fresh perspective on your life by pretending that you're a high-priced consultant who has been called in to assess how to maximise the returns in your life. With a neutral, questioning attitude, analyse what you're doing now and how you're doing it, where the sticking points are, where more or new resources are needed, and so forth.

This could apply to any phase of your life: the outcome could be making a certain amount of money, or having a great relationship with your children, or getting fit, for example. Usually you see your life in the "associated" view – that is, through your own eyes. When you look at it in a "dissociated" state – that is, as though watching it from the outside, as though on a movie screen, suddenly you get a whole different picture. To make this really vivid it helps to stand up, close your eyes, and recreate with all your senses what it would be like to be this other person. If you imagine The Consultant to be taller than you, for example, you might notice your posture shifting. If your image of The Consultant is someone who is less emotional than you, you may feel your mental state turning cooler.

Just like any consultant, note what's working and what isn't, what's needed, what has worked for other people, and then write down your recommendations.

ON ADVICE

"Advice is what we ask for when we already know the answer but wish we didn't." *Erica Jong, Writer*

Then get back into the associated state (in other words, your normal self) and read the report and decide which of the recommendations you want to accept, and begin to implement them. Periodically call in The Consultant to evaluate how things are going and what changes could help. You might even make the first day of each month your appointment with The Consultant in the mirror.

Create your own arch-enemy

Usually it's good to think positively, but sometimes a bit of strategic negative thinking can help, too. Have you noticed how hard people will work when they are fighting an enemy? The more specific the enemy, the better. You can use this power by creating a final variation of an Alter Ego, an arch-enemy who is the symbol of whatever may be holding you back.

Most of the time in reality this is not another person, but some aspect of yourself. For example, if you're trying to lose weight and shape up, most likely it is your own problems with sticking to your diet and exercise regime that get in your way. You can create an image for this "enemy". Maybe you want to imagine Blimpo – a cartoon-like hugely overweight and slobby creature. Blimpo hates it when you exercise or when you resist the lure of chocolates because Blimpo wants to make you into their own image.

Imagine your reaction if, the next time you are tempted, you call Blimpo to mind. Make the right choice and watch Blimpo deflate a little – enjoy the downfall of the enemy! The best thing is this all happens in your imagination. You do not need to tell anyone else about it – all they will notice is that you are doing better than ever before.

By using the Alter Egos, you will have greater control of your own actions. Of course along the way you will have to deal with other people, and the next chapter will equip you to find and work with allies and to negotiate like a master.

Website chapter bonus

At www.focusquick.com you'll find a downloadable visualis-ation that gets you into The Consultant Alter Ego and allows you mentally to rehearse how you might employ them.

8

How to manage other people

So far we've been looking at your patterns of behaviour and techniques you can use on yourself to speed toward achieving your goals, but naturally you are also affected by the behaviour of the people around you. In this chapter you'll find out how to overcome their negativity and gain their support.

We all need support

Not having the support of those closest to you can be a real drag on your efforts. For example, a spouse or partner or parents may be condescending or sceptical about your goals. Can you get them to change their pattern? Well, yes, but only by changing your pattern. There is a very wise saying about this: "We train other people how to treat us."

When the other person makes a joke about your goal, say something like, "Normally I'd try to ignore that kind of comment, but I've decided to tell you how hurtful I find it, whether or not you intend it that way. Now you can decide whether to continue making those kinds of jokes, or to treat my goal with respect because it's important to me."

If you stick to this new behaviour, it's unlikely the other person will continue in the old one, although their first response may be to storm out, or sulk, or do something else not particularly positive. But at least you've broken the old pattern and shown that change is possible. By the way, it's highly likely that that person will try several times to get you back into the previous pattern, so you will have to remain steadfast.

Naturally you must show the same kind of respect for whatever the other person values, even if it's something you don't find appealing yourself, so before you start trying to change others it's worthwhile making sure you haven't been acting the same way. Apologising is never easy but it's a great start if you recognise that you have been partly responsible for the current state of a relationship and want to put it on a different footing.

There is no guarantee that the other person will ever behave exactly the way you want them to, but often a simple change in your part of the pattern will have a positive impact on the other person's behaviour. You can treat this process just as you do your other goals, namely trying different things until you find the one that works.

If there is one person whose support you'd like to gain, write their name here:

_____

What will you say to this person to help them be more supportive?

_____

Why people are negative

Writing in the *Personal & Finance Confidential* newsletter, training expert Dr. Julian Feinstein pointed out that basically the world can be split into positive people – those who expect to win, and negative people – those who expect to be right.

AN ALL-PURPOSE REPLY

US writer and broadcaster Alexander Woollcott always wrote back the same thing to people who took exception to things he said on his radio show: "Dear Sir or Madam, You may be right." That usually stopped the correspondence.

This is a terrific insight: the people who are negative about anything new or unusual often are not actually interested in the thing being undertaken, they are invested in being right. And, because most new things fail, the best way to be right is to be negative. Of course the leaders, the visionaries, and the just plain determined are the ones who stick to something until it does work – which is why they are so annoying to the negative people.

If you do have someone in your life who refuses to overcome their negativity regarding what you are doing, it's best just to ignore them. However, be sure that you have some people in your life who share your enthusiasm and ambitions. If none of your friends are like that, it may be time to look for some additional friends or colleagues. Professional groups, networking groups, and other associations are a great place to meet people like this.

If you think it would be helpful to add some supportive people to your circle of friends, jot down where you think you could meet them:

Do you know what people want?

The secret to getting people to give you what you want is to help them get what they want. What is the number one thing people are after? Day to day, most people are yearning for one simple thing: recognition. We all want to be appreciated, to be seen to be special. We want that from the time we are very small: "Mum, look at me!" and "Dad, see what I can do!" It's just that as we get older we learn how to act cooler and not reveal our desperation for attention as much. If you learn how to give people recognition and you do so consistently, not only will you be perceived as being especially charismatic but you will also find people eager to help you reach your goals.

66We all want to be appreciated, to be seen to be special. 99

The case of the shy student

If you doubt the powerful effect of recognition, let me share with you a story I heard about a young woman who went to see the late therapist, Milton Erickson. He was noted for his unconventional but highly-effective methods, and his techniques went on to become part of the foundations of Neuro Linguistic Programming. A very shy young woman who had just started university went to see Erickson. She was severely depressed and isolated. He gave her a simple prescription: three times a day she was to give her fellow students a genuine compliment. The fact that it had to be genuine meant that she had to pay attention to the other people to search for something she really liked, and also that her comment would not come across as mere flattery.

At the end of three months, she was one of the most popular students on campus, and her depression and isolation were things of the past.

How to give recognition

It's ironic that the thing people want most costs us nothing to give, yet most of us are extremely sparing with it. Maybe we fear that praise or appreciation will sound false, or that by giving to someone else we are somehow diminishing ourselves. That's not true, of course, and if you can overcome your natural reticence you may be amazed at the effect it has on your relationships. Here are some ways to give people the recognition they want.

Learn to really listen

Most of the time when someone is speaking to us, we stop listening about halfway through so that we can begin to come up with our next remark. Instead, focus your attention on what they are saying until they reach the end. You'll still come up with an answer or comment instantly. There's more about this in Chapter 10, which focuses on the extraordinary power of language.

Increase your eye contact

Most people have pretty good eye contact when they are listening to someone else, but not when they are talking themselves. Obviously you want to keep it natural, not some kind of psycho stare, but increasing your eye contact even by 25% will make a big difference. If looking directly into the other person's eyes makes you nervous, either look at the spot right between their eyes, or shift your glance gently back and forth between their left eye and their right eye. However, don't get so caught up in this that you're not registering what they're saying.

Use their name

I'm not suggesting that you do this the way they do in soap operas, where every sentence starts with the other person's name, just that you occasionally find a natural way to slip it into the conversation. The most natural is at the beginning and end, when you are greeting them or saying goodbye. It's a cliché but also true that one of our favourite sounds is that of our own name.

Give genuine compliments

It can be how well they're looking, an item of clothing, something they did recently, or anything else. If you mean it, it won't sound false, even though it may still feel that way until you get used to doing this. You don't have to go overboard,

It is possible to overdo eye contact.

either. It can be a simple comment like, "Those are great shoes", or "That was a good point you made in the meeting, it really helped move things along."

FISHING FOR COMPLIMENTS

If you have trouble coming up with compliments, take a few minutes to consider what kinds of comments make you feel good. What kinds of compliments do you treasure? The same things will work for everyone.

Notice and comment on it when someone does something you wanted them to do

Studies with animals and people show that we are very similar in one way: behaviour that is rewarded tends to happen again. With animals the reward is treats, with humans a compliment or acknowledgement is enough. This is by far the most effective way of shaping someone else's behaviour. This has been shown in sometimes humorous ways. In one psychology class the students decided to test this theory with their professor. The sessions took place in a large lecture hall and the professor was in the habit of walking back and forth across the stage. Whenever he walked to the left, the students gave him their full attention. Whenever he walked to the right, they stopped looking at him so much, leaned back in their chairs and otherwise showed a lack of interest. By the end of a couple of lectures, the professor stayed rooted to the left end of the stage – without ever noticing what he was doing or why.

Ask for advice

People love to solve other people's problems – maybe because it takes attention off their own. When you ask for advice you're implying that you value the other person's intelligence and experience, which is a rewarding feeling for them. Just be sure that you select issues on which you are willing to take their advice, at least some of the time, and always acknowledge your gratitude for their guidance.

Say thanks

Again, don't wait for some momentous thing, it can be as simple as "Thanks for backing me up in the meeting, it made my job a lot easier", or "Thanks for giving me the chance to design your website, I know we're going to come up with something special."

Use pen and paper

In this age of email a written note or letter really stands out. A study at Wake Forest University in the United States took at look at how much weight members of Congress gave to emails. The answer: very little. They put them almost on the same level as petitions and mass mailings. What impressed them more was a personal letter (a personal visit was even more powerful). Whether you're writing to a valued friend, trying to sell someone on a new idea, or making a business contact, consider what the impact would be of a personal letter, maybe typed or printed, but with a handwritten postscript.

Which strategies will you use?

Below, put a check mark by the strategies you plan to implement now:

❏ Listening more carefully

❏ Increasing eye contact

❏ Using the other person's name more

❏ Giving more compliments

❏ Reinforcing desired behaviour

❏ Asking for advice

❏ Saying thanks more often

❏ Using written messages

What is one situation in which you can use one or more of these within the next 24 hours?

_____

_____

_____

Start a mutual admiration society

One variation of giving recognition is especially powerful – and kind of sneaky. In a February 2002 article in *Fast Company* magazine, Harriet Rubin told the following story. Two women in the Polish military are said to have made a secret pact: they would help each other to rise in the hierarchy. When Magda went to a meeting, she would be sure to work praise of Theresa into the discussion. Whenever Theresa wrote a report, she would recommend Magda for new responsibilities.

DOING SOMETHING DIFFERENT

For more examples of creative ways that people have made their business or service stand out, see the 100 case studies in my book, *Do Something Different*, published by Virgin Books.

Before long, third parties were saying, "I hear Theresa is brilliant" or "Magda is being considered for such-and-such a position".

Consider finding someone whose work you genuinely admire and make a similar pact. Naturally this works best in situations in which you are not directly in competition and when the pact remains private and not too obvious.

Who is one person you might consider for this kind of relationship?

All of the techniques in this chapter have one thing in common: they create a win-win situation for you and the people whose support or help you need in order to realise your dreams. Another way to achieve great results is to focus the language you use with others as well as with yourself, and that's what you'll learn in the next chapter.

Website chapter bonus

At www.focusquick.com you will find an interview with a top animal trainer about how the same principles apply to "training" animals and people.

9

How to focus your language for extraordinary results

In the last chapter you read about a number of ways to get people to cooperate in helping you reach your goals. Being persuasive is a crucial skill and the strongest persuasion tools are your words. This is another skill you already have, but perhaps are not fully aware of how to use it consistently. By the time you've finished reading this chapter, you'll know how to apply this skill whenever you need it.

You're already a persuasive communicator

If you doubt that you already have the ability to use focused language, consider:

● Have you ever convinced your parents that you were just at a friend's house, studying, when actually you were (fill in the blank)?

● Have you ever convinced anyone to go out with you? To marry you?

● Have you ever stopped a child who was about to do something dangerous?

- Have you ever been the winning candidate in a job interview?

In those kinds of situations we all tend to be persuasive because we are very clear and focused on the outcome we want. Instinctively we establish rapport with the other person and use whatever approach we feel will be most likely to succeed. By learning how to focus more of your communication like this, you will gain a powerful success tool.

The problem with most conversations

We like to think of conversations as exchanges in which we listen to the other person and share our thoughts and feelings with them. It should be easy, yet often we leave a conversation or business meeting feeling frustrated that the other person didn't seem to understand. The other person leaves feeling the same way. Why is it so difficult?

One problem is that we tend to ignore the reality of human communication. Let's take an example: George and Bill are colleagues. They run into each other at the water cooler on Monday morning, and George notices that Bill has a bit of a tan.

George: Hey, Bill, got some sun, eh?
Bill: Yes, Jane and I took the boys to the lake. First time we've been camping together this—

At this point, George has heard the trigger word "camping" and starts to think about what he wants to say on the subject. The fact that Bill is still talking is convenient, because it gives George time to think.

Bill: ... other than the outside toilets, ha ha. But—

George is ready. He interrupts.

George: I used to go camping all the time when I was young. My dad was a Scout Master, so we could—

Bill is slightly annoyed that George has interrupted – after all, Bill hasn't gotten around to telling him yet about the fish he caught. Oh well, George will have to take a breath some-time…

George:—all those merit badges, I still have them somewhere, I'm not sure where. (He takes a breath)

Bill is more diplomatic than George, so he decides to make a link between what George has just been saying and what he wants to say:

Bill: You must have done a bit of fishing in the Scouts, eh? This weekend, I caught—

And so it will go on. Most conversations are not a dialogue, but intersecting monologues. You are the star of your own life, and the others are merely supporting actors. Of course in the other person's life, they are the star, and you are merely the supporting player. We're all working from different scripts. No wonder communication can be difficult!

“We're all working from different scripts. No wonder communication can be difficult!”

Let's look at some ways you can use language and associated behaviours to communicate more successfully. In each case, I'll give concrete examples, because "communication" is an abstract word – it only really takes on meaning when you know what you want to communicate, and to whom. Once you know that, you can decide which "how" will work best. These techniques work in family life, friendships, coun-selling, and business. As you read, you might like to consider

THE MYTH OF MARS AND VENUS

In recent years it has been accepted that women talk more and interrupt less often than men. Also that women talk more about feelings and relationships while men talk more about facts, and that women's conversation tends to be cooperative while men's tends to be competitive. However, when psychologist Dr. Janet Hyde, of the University of Wisconsin in Madison, conducted a meta-analysis of studies of male–female communications she found that there is very little difference in the quantity and quality of male and female talk.

("The Gender Similarities Hypothesis", American Psychologist, September 2005).

in which areas of your life it will help you the most to use them.

Make a connection with the secret of rapport

One of the common phrases people use to indicate there is a rapport between them and another person is to say, "We are on the same wavelength." When there is this kind of connection between you, it's much more likely that the other person will do what you want them to do. While we seem to connect automatically with some people, it's also a skill you can learn and use to your advantage.

Research reveals that rapport seems to be based primarily on similarity or the perception of similarity. The similarity may only be in the area that applies to the situation at hand. The person you enjoy going to football games with because you share a fanatical interest in sports, for example, may not share your interest in old movies; but while you're at the game or discussing football, you two have great rapport.

As this implies, you can establish rapport by finding an interest in common with the other person. And what is each person's greatest interest most of the time? That's right: themselves. Therefore, you can establish rapport with just about anyone by taking a genuine interest in them. Let me stress the word "genuine". A real interest is much more rewarding to both parties than a feigned one. Besides, in my experience only psychopaths and actors are really good at faking it.

When are the times you might want to establish rapport? Often it's when you're meeting someone new and you want them to be receptive to your message. Your message might be that you find them attractive and want to go out with them, or that you have a wonderful product they should buy.

LEARNING TO LISTEN

If you find it difficult to really listen, try the following:

- In your mind, paraphrase what the other person is saying.

- Rather than trying to formulate an answer, try to assess how the person feels about what they are saying.

- Set yourself a period of time, maybe just five minutes to start with, to listen intensively. Gradually increase the periods until it becomes automatic.

In all situations, there tends to be a "breaking the ice" period, and this is when establishing rapport is most important. First, break the pattern illustrated in our sample conversation between Bill and George, by actually listening. Instead of letting trigger words send you into yourself (at which point you will be only half-listening), stay with the conversation. Hear the words, but also watch the other person for non-verbal clues to how they feel about what is being described. Give feedback, both verbal and non-verbal (head nodding, smiling, etc.) to show that you understand and are in synch.

Once you start really listening, it's not as hard as it used to be to find the other person of genuine interest. Let's use the example of meeting a potential client. Shift your focus from your own desire to sell to wanting to understand the person you are dealing with. Ask some questions and listen to the answers. If there is a good match between what they need and what you're offering, it will be a natural progression to talk about your product or services.

Establish greater rapport by matching their language

Listening will also give you useful information for a rapport strategy that comes from the field of NLP (Neuro Linguistic Programming). The technique is to match the person with whom you are dealing. One of the things you can match is the language they use to represent their world.

The main representation categories are **visual** (pictures), **auditory** (sounds), and **kinaesthetic** (feeling). If you listen to someone talk, you will find that they tend to use words from one of these categories more than from the others.

A visual person will say things like, "That's clear" or "I see your point" or "Give me some time to look at that."

An auditory person will say things like, "I heard what you're saying" or "That rings a bell" or "I like the sound of that."

A kinaesthetic person will say things like, "I have a rough idea" or "Those are pretty heavy numbers" or "My gut instinct is that you're right."

Most people will use a mixture and some will also use phrases that are gustatory – relating to taste – or olfactory – relating to smell, but typically one of the above three predominates. For practice, you can listen for these when watching TV interviews.

If you then match the other person by using language with the same orientation, the two of you will be more in synch. If addressing a group, use all the categories; if you use only your own favourite one, some of your listeners will not feel on the same wavelength.

Practise using the representational systems

To see, tune into, or get a feeling for this, take a moment to consider your own preferences. If you're not sure, mentally describe something or explain something you do. You'll soon notice some terms that tip you off as to which of the categories you prefer. Write down your preferred representational system (visual, auditory, or kinaesthetic):

Now repeat the description in your mind but this time work in some terms that come from one of the other two primary systems. For example, let's say you're primarily visual and your

George is primarily auditory.

first description is something like, "When working with a new client, I try to see what they really want from the process." If you then switch to using auditory terms, you might instead say something like, "When working with a new client, I listen for what they really want from the process." If you switch to kinaesthetic mode, it could be, "I try to get in touch with what they really want." Jot down your alternatives here:

Alternative one:

_____

Alternative two:

_____

Guiding a conversation by pacing and leading

There is another NLP language concept, pacing and leading, that is useful in establishing rapport and also in helping change a negative conversation into a positive one. Let's take a personal example: a friend calls you up and the conversation goes like this:

Other person: "I'm so depressed!"

You: "Cheer up! The sun is shining, the birds are singing, you should be happy to be alive!!"

Not likely to be effective, is it? When you counter one extreme with another extreme, there is no change. If anything, the other extreme just gets more extreme. In our example, the other person now has another reason to be depressed: you are totally insensitive to their feelings. Let's try it again:

Other person: "I'm so depressed!"

You (sympathetic tone of voice): "What's the matter?"

Other person: "I've gained back two pounds this week. I'm such a weakling!"

You: "Dieting is so difficult."

Other person: "I had three business dinners last week, that's what did it."

You: "Hmmm, yeah, it's hard not to eat the same things everybody else is eating. Any business dinners next week?"

Other person: "Only one. I'm taking out a potential client."

You: "Japanese food can be pretty healthy and light in calories. Do you think they might agree to a Japanese restaurant?"

Other person: "Good idea. I can ask."

This is a bit compressed, but you can see the pattern. You start out by expressing empathy with your tone of voice as well as your words. Then you look for a genuinely more positive aspect to focus on (in this case it's that there's only one business dinner next week; in real life, it may take a bit longer to find the positive aspect). Then you move forward into looking at some useful alternatives. At times, this last step may not be necessary; the other person may already have alternatives and the only thing needed is a little sympathy.

> ### PERFECTING YOUR PACING
>
> If you have trouble pacing someone's mood, try matching their posture and how they hold their heads (subtly, of course). Then very gradaully change your posture to more closely match the mood you'd like to encourage in the other person. If you do it well, they will also begin to change their posture.

Here's another brief example, this time a sales situation:

Customer: "These cars are all too expensive."
Salesperson: "Not really. They're excellent value!"

Again, not likely to succeed.

Here's an alternative:

Customer: "These care are all too expensive."
Salesperson: "It seems like everything is costing more, doesn't it?"
Customer: "I'm going to have find something cheaper."
Salesperson: "Frankly, that might be a good idea, in the short term. These cars will only save you money in the long run."
Customer: "What do you mean?"

Then the salesperson might discuss depreciation figures, fuel consumption, the financing plan or whatever else makes the car excellent value.

First you establish that you're a friendly force who understands their predicament. Then you gradually refocus the conversation. Watch for signs that you're going too fast for their comfort. If so, backtrack a step, pace them where they are, and then take a smaller step forward. Eventually you will bring them around to a version of the conversation that supports your goal.

Persuade through the power of reframing

Reframing means looking at something in a different way. It's similar to using metaphors and stories, in that the reframed version is like a new story about the same thing. For instance, if the glass is half empty, it must also be half full. Here's an example of reframing in a conversation:

Maria: "There's a personal development workshop my sister has been raving about, and it's on again this weekend. Do you think you might want to go?"

Ted: "I don't know. Where is it? And when?"

Maria: "This weekend. It's in Birmingham. We'd have to leave London at 6 am."

Ted: "Be up at 6 am on a Saturday?! Forget it!"

Maria: "Yes, that's pretty early. Of course it would only be the one morning, and the weekend could change your life."

Ted: "Change my life? How?"

The trigger word here was 6 am. Probably Ted immediately made an internal picture of trying to get up at 5 am and didn't like it. Then Maria reframed it by putting it in a different, much bigger context: getting up early one day to change one's life. That was enough to make Ted interested again and ask for more information.

An example parents will be familiar with is a young child saying she doesn't want to go to school. You may be able to reframe the idea of getting up by saying something like, "I bet the other kids will be having fun today in art class, doing finger painting. And I guess your best friend Susie will be OK on her own at lunch – she'll probably find somebody else to play with." Suddenly the need to get up is part of a much bigger picture and will be more appealing.

> **REFRAMING WITH QUANTITY**
>
> One of the typical ways that advertisers use reframing is to describe something large in terms of small chunks ("costs no more than a cup of coffee per day"), or something small in terms of a larger aggregate ("by the end of the year your savings will allow you to buy Christmas presents for the whole family"). If you are trying to persuade someone of something that involves a quantity of time or money, consider which way of framing it will be more effective.

Reframing practice

Think of one example of something you'd like to persuade someone else about. It could be a personal or business situation. Jot it down here:

_____

Now think of one way you could reframe this that would make it more appealing to the person you're trying to convince:

_____

Focus your communication with metaphors and stories

All of the great religious works, like the Bible, use metaphors and parables to make their points. Telling a story can be extremely powerful. Let me give you an example – my favourite Zen story:

An elderly monk and a novice were walking through the countryside. They came to a raging river and saw there a young woman who was afraid to cross. The elderly monk took her upon his shoulders and carried her across. She thanked him profusely and they went their separate ways. For the next three days, the young monk was disturbed, and he became more and more agitated. Finally the old monk asked him what was the matter. "Master," he said, "you know we are forbidden to have physical contact with women!" "Ah," said the old monk, "that woman at the river. I put her down three days ago ... are you still carrying her?"

I defy anyone to come up with a more elegant and powerful way to make the point!

The great thing about a metaphor is that the listener has to make sense of it, to relate it to their life or the situation being discussed. Often this happens on the subconscious level and thus goes more deeply into their awareness.

Public speakers have long used metaphors and metaphorical stories (check the speeches of Abraham Lincoln, Winston Churchill, or any of the great orators), and metaphors are still powerful because they are entertaining as well as informative.

A metaphor need not be a whole story, it can be simply a phrase or a sentence. Let's say a colleague feels that negotiations have hit a standstill and there's no point in going on. You could say something like, "Yeah, it feels like we're hitting a brick wall. I wonder if there's a way to tunnel under it." Just a simple statement like that may give your colleague the idea not to stick to the same strategy, but to consider trying something different.

The next time you need to make a point but feel that making it directly might lead to resistance, construct a metaphor and drop that into your conversation instead. Avoid the temptation to follow the metaphor with your explanation of what it means, or else you'll negate its value.

Practise with a metaphor

Think of a message you'd like to get across (it can be the same one you used when practising with representational systems or a new one). Write it down here:

_____

Now think of a metaphor, a story, or just a phrase, that might make the situation easier for someone else to understand or relate to. If you have trouble thinking of one, consider whether a well-known folk or fairy tale might give you some material. "The Three Little Pigs" is about preparation, for example, and "Goldilocks and the Three Bears" is about finding just the right solution. Write it down here:

_____

_____

_____

Defuse opposition with the Three Questions technique

Naturally you will sometimes encounter opposition to your ideas. The goal of the "Three Questions" technique is to prevent opposition from hardening too quickly and to give you information you can use either as a basis for changing your own position or for bringing the other person around to yours.

This technique is simple: before opposing any statement by another person, ask at least three questions.

Let's run through an example of a screenwriter in a meeting with a producer:

Producer: "The ending of your script doesn't work for me."
Writer: "Everything in that script leads up to that ending!"
Producer: "Yes, but it doesn't work."
Writer: "You're the first person to say that! Everybody else loves the ending."

I'm probably creating a stroppier writer here than producers normally encounter. But you can see that this is a familiar pattern and that it isn't getting them anywhere. Let's see how three questions might help:

Producer: "The ending of your script doesn't work for me."
Writer: "I see. What, specifically, do you feel doesn't work?"
Producer: "I just don't think the woman would act that way."
Writer: "Hmm, that's interesting. What does she do that you don't find plausible?"
Producer: "She picks up the gun and goes out onto the street – I mean, how does she suddenly know how to use a gun?"

Writer: "I see, so you feel that we haven't laid the groundwork for that action?"

Producer: "That's right!"

Writer: "Well, maybe there's something we can do earlier in the script to set up that she's able to use a gun – maybe her father used to take her hunting, or she did a self-defence course or something like that."

You may be surprised at how often what the other person says first isn't really what they mean. Asking at least three questions will help you get to the bottom of their meaning, and then you can respond to that. Also, asking three questions stops it from immediately turning into a battle. You will come across as very reasonable, and that in itself may be helpful in further discussion.

How to break a block

There are times when, with all the goodwill in the world, you will find that you and the person with whom you're speaking just can't agree on some point. What to do then? Move up one or more levels to the point where you do agree, and then generate additional alternatives. In other words, move the focus of the conversation away from the point of disagreement, to a point of agreement, then on to a new point of agreement.

Let's take a business example: your firm's PR agency made a mess of a campaign. You want to fire them and bring the function in-house while your colleague wants to give them a strong reprimand but give them another chance.

Backing up one step, what was the last thing you agreed upon? Perhaps it was just that the PR company did a very poor job and didn't liaise closely enough with your company before releasing information to the press.

Now start generating alternatives that would deal with the problem that you do agree needs to be dealt with: maybe you could set up a formal system of clearing information; maybe you could ask one of the PR company employees to work from your premises; maybe you could assign one of your employees to liaise daily with them, or put them on their premises. You generate responses to the problem until you find one that is acceptable to both of you.

The other benefit of this technique is that by stepping back to a level on which you do agree, you defuse the hostility that can be present when two people are both defending their ground.

You say yes so they say no (how to cope with polarity response)

Anybody who has had dealings with a four-year-old already understands the concept of polarity response. It means that whatever you say, the other person will automatically say the opposite. It's a strategy for rebelling and testing limits; most people go through it when they're three or four and again when they're teenagers, but some stick with it all their lives.

I once worked with a woman who had the most extreme example of polarity response (combined with general nega-tivism) that I've ever encountered. No matter what anybody proposed, she was against it and could instantly generate 22 reasons why it would never work. We eventually discovered a constructive alternative to killing her! We realised she was actually a good source of information about what might go wrong with our plans. Among those 22 reasons, there were a few that were not just general paranoia but were actually valid, and if we headed those off we could strengthen our plans.

Notice what happened: we reframed our perception of her from being a negative doom-sayer to being someone who could give us some valuable information. This changed our relationship with her (not to say that she wasn't still annoying . . .) and helped our work. This is a good example of how reframing isn't just about image or feelings – it can have a concrete result.

In some cases, however, you need to get someone who has habitual polarity response to agree to something. How can you do it? Here are two strategies:

1. Give them several alternatives, all of which would be acceptable to you, and ask them to choose one. They'll probably hate all of them but you can still get them to choose the least objectionable.

2. Take the position opposite to, or at least different from, the one you really support. The other person will oppose it and you can let them convince you. Don't give in too easily, though. A friend used this when she was visiting a relative in hospital who responded negatively to any positive statement (e.g., "You're looking better today" would lead her to say, "Oh, but I feel much worse"). Finally my friend started being even more negative than the patient ("You look at death's door today!") which shocked the patient into protesting that she didn't feel that bad.

Focus your self-talk

Equally as important as what you say to others is what you say to yourself. Most of us have an internal running commentary. Often this is shockingly judgemental and harsh. We say things to ourselves we would never say to a friend or colleague. Just as you can now listen more attentively to what others say, you can begin to pay more attention to what you say to yourself – and to challenge it when it is harsh or otherwise not constructive. You can use many of the same techniques you've read about in this chapter. For example, when you make a mistake, rather than getting down on yourself for it, reframe it. Put it into perspective with everything else you've done. Making a mistake does not make you a dummy or a failure – it makes you a human being. We all make them, and when we realise we've made them we have the opportunity to choose between punishing ourselves or simply learning something.

Think back to a time recently when you made a mistake. What did you say to yourself about it? If you can't remember, you can still make an educated guess:

_____

Would it have been more constructive to say something else? If so, write it here:

_____

Making this change permanent requires some practice. A few times a day check what you're saying to yourself and immediately correct anything that is harsh. Over time you will create a new habit of listening to a constructive inner guide rather than a harsh inner critic.

All of the techniques in this chapter work best when you know what you want to communicate and when you respect the other person's reality. Then the stage is set for you to focus the communication in the way that helps you achieve your goals. One of the things that makes it hard to focus is information overload. In the next chapter, you will discover techniques for taming that phenomenon.

Website chapter bonus

At www.focusquick.com you will find a video interview with communication expert and therapist Philip Harland about how to communicate more effectively with others and yourself using a technique called "clean language".

10 CHAPTER TEN

How to create information focus

One of the biggest problems that plagues creative people, who are naturally curious and tend to seek and take in lots of ideas, is information overload. It is very easy to be overwhelmed by all the input that comes from television, radio, magazines, newspapers, and especially the internet. Learning how to deal with what seems to be an ever-increasing flood is vital if you are to focus your effort where it will have most value. In this chapter you'll find tools that will help you focus on the information you need and ignore the rest.

❝focus on the information you need and ignore the rest.❞

You are receiving evermore information

In 1990 information architect Richard Saul Wurman wrote a book called *Information Anxiety*. His central point was that we are inundated with information. The striking example he cited is that a weekday edition of the *New York Times* contains more information than the average person was likely to come across in a lifetime in seventeenth-century England. When Wurman was writing, the internet had not yet developed into a fountain that dwarfs every other information source ever invented.

Of course it's wonderful that we have so much information so easily accessible. The problem is that we have to figure out what is trustworthy and what is propaganda or misinformation, what is current and what is outdated, and what is relevant to our challenges at a given point.

> "Everybody gets so much information all day long that they lose their common sense."
>
> Gertrude Stein (1874–1946)

A 2003 study reported in the *Journal of Personality and Social Psychology* reveals that creative people are poor at shutting out irrelevant information. At the extreme level this is linked with mental illness but at a milder level it could be possible that such people are creative exactly because they can see how information that is seemingly irrelevant may actually relate to a problem. Nonetheless, this tendency can make it hard to concentrate and therefore could work against you.

Noise = unwanted information

The advent of the cubicle culture has increased the noise level at our workplace. It's now hard to find any public place that doesn't feature music playing, TV screens flashing, and half a dozen other bids for your attention. Some bus stops and billboards are voice-activated and call out their sales messages to you as you pass by. Even many of London's black cabs have TV screens playing adverts to grab your attention for the few minutes you might otherwise have let your thoughts wander as you glance at the streets. All of this is information even if it's not information you want.

Studies have shown that children living near airports or busy highways have lower reading scores. According to Dr. Alice H. Suter, an audiologist at the US National Institute for Occupational Safety and Health: "Included in noise-related problems are high blood pressure, peptic ulcers, cardiovascular deaths, strokes, suicides, degradation of the immune system, and impairment of learning. Noise is also associated with an increase in aggression and a decrease in cooperation."

If you find you sometimes have to work in public spaces, such as at a train station while waiting for your train or in a coffee shop between appointments, one great tool to carry with you is noise-cancelling headphones. I originally bought these to use on airplanes, to reduce the drone of the engines and other unwanted noise. You can plug them into the airplane's entertainment system, and you'll get much better sound than on the airline's cheap headphones. You can also wear them (unplugged) anytime and anywhere that you want to reduce

Simon is determined to avoid information overload.

distracting noise. If you feel self-conscious, just tuck the plug into your pocket and people will assume you're listening to an MP3 player. Another, lower-tech option: earplugs.

You can also make it a point to find cafés, libraries, or other places that don't play music and provide a generally quiet atmosphere. If you make a habit of working in quiet places you may be surprised at how much calmer and more productive you are.

Changing your environment to allow focus

What could you do to make your working environment more conducive to concentration?

_____

_____

What are two or three places you could take refuge in if your working environment becomes too stressful?

_____

_____

_____

How to consume information with a purpose in mind

Information becomes overwhelming when you consume it with no particular end in mind. If you start with a purpose you automatically develop filters that help you sort out what is relevant and what is extraneous. A good example is the huge amount of email most people receive. There is some that is personal and requires your attention, there is some that is spam and can be deleted quickly, but the problem mail is the rest. The 80/20 principle applies once again: most likely only 20% of these messages apply to your most important goals. The other 80% may be interesting in a general sense but not directly relevant. We will look more closely at how to deal with email in Chapter 12, but for now here are four strategies you can apply to it as well as to information coming from other sources:

- Before you look at the source of information, quickly remind yourself of the topics of greatest interest to you at this point, the ones that relate to your most important goals.

- If you know that this information is not relevant, don't even look at it – either discard it or put it aside for a time when the information it contains may be more relevant.

- When possible, delegate the review of this material to someone else. Tell them what information you are looking for. They can highlight, photocopy, or scan the relevant bits for your review.

- For the information that you do look at, scan it for the most important points rather than reading it all. Use chapter titles, headings and subheadings, topic sentences, underlined or boldface words, and end of chapter key points to guide you to the content that is most relevant.

Too many magazines? If you have a backlog of magazines, just look through the table of contents and go directly to any articles that may be pertinent. If there aren't any, dump the magazine without reading it.

If, like me, you really enjoy finding interesting bits of information on the internet, this may sound like harsh advice but it applies only to your work time. If you wish to spend some of your free time browsing magazines or the internet without any particular aim, that's still an option.

Get information from reliable sources

These days anybody can create a website, blog, or podcast (an audio or video program delivered over the internet) in minutes and present dubious information as facts, or represent themselves as authorities when actually they don't have any relevant education or experience. In other cases they may be well qualified, but the underlying hidden intention of their information is to sell you something or convert you to a particular viewpoint. When you are going to rely on a source it's worthwhile doing some checking as to its background and reliability. One of the benefits of search engines is that they make it fairly easy to cross-check information with a variety of sources rather than relying on just one. If the information is important, do double-check facts before you take any action based on them.

Know and apply your learning style

People learn in different ways. Some like to read, some like to hear lectures, some need to experience something before they can master it. These days almost every kind of information is available in every kind of format. For instance, if you want to learn how to use a software program you can read a manual or you can listen to and watch a video lesson (like the ones available at www.lynda.com) or you can attend a class in which you get hands-on experience. If you haven't looked into the alternatives lately, you may be surprised, for example, at how much information is now available in the form of audio books and podcasts, video podcasts, and instructional DVDs.

If you are not using the format that works best for you, coping with instructional information becomes a chore and takes extra time. One of the reasons I've augmented this book with so many bonuses on the website is that there I can give you information in the form of audio and video interviews and visualisations that will appeal to your other ways of learning.

If there is something you need to learn in order to help you reach your goal, check out all the possible methods and use those that best match your preferences.

How connected do you need to be?

The stereotype of the successful businessperson is someone who is connected to a mobile phone 24/7. But is that the reality? *Fortune* magazine asked some peak performers for the secrets of their success. Here's part of what Bill Gross, the Chief Investment Officer of fixed income investor PIMCO, said: "I don't have a cell phone, I don't have a Blackberry. My motto is, I don't want to be connected – I want to be disconnected." He added that the most important part of his day is the hour and a half of yoga and exercise he does first thing every morning.

> "Life is what happens to you while you're busy making other plans."
> *John Lennon (1940–1980)*

If you don't have any disconnected time during the day, or any time when you exercise, maybe it would be a good idea to start. If it works for a man who is directly responsible for $200 billion in investments, it could work for you!

Here, in short form, are other methods you can use to disconnect in order to have time to think:

- Use an answering machine. You can indicate the time that you'll be answering the phone again and when you'll be returning calls.
- Check phone messages only two or three times a day.
- Make all your phone calls one right after the other.
- Keep a phone log so it's easy to find numbers you've called previously.
- Avoid call-waiting (it only allows you to annoy two people at once).
- Decide which messages could be more quickly and easily answered with a brief email.
- Tell long-winded callers you have a meeting in five minutes.
- Get out of the office during lunch and turn off your mobile.
- At home, turn off your mobile at mealtimes (and the rest of the time, too, if possible).

When do you disconnect?

List the times during your work hours that you disconnect, even if just for a few minutes:

_____

What are some other times you might be able to disconnect in order to have some stress-free thinking time?

_____

_____

Of the strategies mentioned above, which ones will you start to integrate into how you work?

_____

_____

_____

By applying the methods in this chapter, you will be able to winnow the 80% of information that is assaulting you but isn't valuable to you, and to create enough quiet time to focus on and absorb the 20% that is. In the next chapter you'll discover strategies for coping with the distracting mountains of paperwork that confront most of us.

Website chapter bonus

At www.focusquick.com you'll find a video interview with journalist and information specialist Rupert Widdicombe about processing information effectively.

11

How to conquer the paper mountain

In the previous chapter you learned strategies for dealing with information overload. By focusing on what you really want to achieve you now have a filter for the torrent of information that comes your way every day and a method for making sure that the 80% that is not relevant doesn't overwhelm you. In this chapter we take that process one giant step further by showing you how to handle the mountain of paperwork that now is also a challenge almost everyone faces.

Are you messy—and so what?

Do you have a messy desk and office with piles of paper everywhere? If so, is that wrong? Well, to steal a question from US television's Dr. Phil, "How's that working for you?" If you are able to find what you need when you need it, it doesn't really matter how messy your office is. However, many messy types (including me) discover that at some point our creative chaos has got out of control and putting our hands on what we need has become a problem. A 2004 study conducted for NEC-Mitsubishi concluded that cluttered desks contribute to worker sickness. Of the 2000 employees they interviewed, 40% said they were infuriated by their cluttered desks but couldn't be bothered to do anything about it and 35% said they had neck or back pain from sitting awkwardly.

> "We can lick gravity, but sometimes the paperwork is overwhelming."
>
> *Wernher von Braun, Rocket Scientist (1912–1977)*

If the state of your desk is a problem most likely it's a function of how you handle paperwork, the lack of a coherent filing system, and the need to be more systematic about handling paper-related tasks. However, if you happen to be a right-brain creative type, you need different solutions from the ones you'll find in most time management or organising books.

How do you like to work?

To find out whether you are more right-brain or left-brain in the context of dealing with paperwork and organising your work, look at the two lists below. Which one is closer to how you like to work?

The *left-brain* type:

- Likes to work on one project at a time.
- Files papers in filing cabinets and is up to date with the filing.
- Follows to do lists by order of priority.
- Uses electronic organisers to keep track of appointments, etc.
- Has no problem staying on schedule and is seldom late.

The *right-brain* type:

- Likes to work on several projects at a time.
- Has piles of papers all over the place.
- Is usually behind with the filing, and prefers to have folders where they can be seen.
- Uses slips of paper or notes to keep track of appointments, etc.
- Tends to miss deadlines and is often late.

As you already know from our chapter on focusing on your strengths, if you are a right-brain type, trying to change yourself into a left-brain type is counterproductive. Whichever of these is closest to describing you, there are tools and methods that are suited to your preferences. Because most books don't feature systems and strategies that right-brain types like, this chapter favours those a bit more, but there's something here for everyone.

New strategies for handling paperwork

"Handle each piece of paper only once." That's the advice you get in every traditional book on time management. I've never found this rule of left-brain time management realistic. Yes, it's a good idea to consider right away whether the piece of paper you are handling can be:

- Thrown away (the best option, when appropriate).
- Filed.
- Passed on to someone else for action.

If it's to be filed, put a Post-It note on it with the name of the file in which it belongs – that means you won't have to make that decision twice.

If it's to be passed on to someone else for action, put a Post-It note on it indicating why you're giving it to them.

In my experience that leaves plenty of other pieces of paper left over. There may be letters you can't answer until you find out something else, ads for a product you may want to buy but you're not sure yet, a notice of a social event you might want to go to, but you have to check with someone else, and so on.

Your new strategy

Jot down on a Post-It note what action you need to take, stick it on the piece of paper, and then put it in a pile. If it's a bill or something else that has the potential to cause trouble, put it in a different pile from everything else and make sure that pile gets attention first. When you go through the piles again one week later, your Post-It notes will quickly tell you what you need to do. Some will no longer be relevant and you can throw them out, some can now be acted upon because you have more information, others need a little longer in a stack.

I'm sure this system would give many left-brainers a heart attack, but it works.

Filing: why you may hate filing cabinets

Many creative people hate using filing cabinets because we're visually oriented, and we like to see where things are. When they're hidden away in a filing cabinet we can't see them and it makes us uneasy.

Your new strategy

Use box files. You can write the name of the file on the side of the box, and keep the box files on your shelves. This is good for when there are a lot of documents. For smaller amounts, you can use folders that have a fold-over flap, and write the name on the top near edge of the flap, making it easily visible.

Also, filing cabinets and their folders make everything look the same and kind of drab. We tend to like colours and to be able to tell things apart visually.

Your new strategy

Use colour-coded file folders or box files. For example, green for financial, blue for reference, red for correspondence.

A filing system that works

For a long time for my writing I used folders with flaps and organised them by categories like "Feature Films", "TV Movies", "Sitcoms", "Dramas", "Non-fiction Books", etc. The problem was that eventually there were a lot of folders in some sections, so that finding a particular file meant going through a lot of folders.

Instead, now each of the main sections gets a letter. For example, A is for Feature Films, B is for TV Movies, C is for Sitcoms, D is for Non-fiction Books and so on (which letter goes with which category is totally arbitrary, and if you run out of letters, you can go to AA, BB, etc.). The examples I'm using relate to files about writing projects but of course you can adapt this so the categories are relevant to your work.

Each folder within a category gets a number added to the letter. So the sections look like this:

A: Feature Films (this is the category title)

A1. *Superbob* (this is the title of a project that fits within this category)

A2. *Mad!*

A3. *Coming Apart*

A4. *Million Dollar Dog*

A5. *Switch*

The next category, TV Movies, gets the next letter:

B: TV Movies

B1: *Would I Lie to You?*

B2: *The Fish and the Bicycle*

B3: *At Sea*

The next category, Sitcoms, gets the letter C:

C: Sitcoms

C1: *Hot Spot*

C2: *What You Wish For*

C3: *Strange Life*

When it's time to make a new folder, it gets the appropriate letter and the next number within that category. So that you don't have to go through all the folders each time you're looking for a file, you make up a master list that you keep handy. If, for instance, I'm looking for the script of my sitcom project, my list will show it's in folder C3 and I can easily locate it on the shelf. I keep the master list in my drawer as well as on the computer, and my assistant also has a copy. We update it by hand as we go along and then once a month or so print out an updated version as well.

The only drawback to this system is that once in a while, when a category gets too full, everything will have to be shifted down the shelves a bit.

Filing instruction booklets

Have you had this experience? You get some new technological marvel, maybe a printer or a digital camera or an MP3 player, and somewhere down the line, maybe a few months after you bought it, something goes wrong and you need the instruction manual. The problem is that you have no idea where it is. Then you start a frustrating, time-wasting search for it, or go on the internet hoping that the manufacturer's website may have a copy online.

The bright folks at Verco, who make office seating, had a great idea: their Maya range of chairs comes with a pocket under the seat where the instructions can be kept permanently. You can adapt this idea by taping a plastic envelope underneath or near the machines or gadgets you use the most (fax machines, copy machines, printers, etc.) to make sure the instructions do not go astray.

Use the focusing power of lists

There is one kind of paperwork you may not be using enough, and that is lists. For everything you need to do that requires some thought, you should have a list to help you do it more quickly. One example is packing for a business trip. Most likely you're going to need the same things every time, so why not make a list to work from and speed up the process? You could even delegate the packing to someone else. Here is part of my master list:

socks	flyer cards
t-shirts	Oyster card for tube
underwear	driver's licence
hankies	address book
trousers	diary
shoes	office kit
shirts	highlighter
sports jacket	accordion wall file
overcoat	business cards
jumper	mobile phone
swimming trunks	phone charger
watch	laptop
trip itinerary	disk driver
tickets	adapter for laptop
passport	disks (incl. projects to work on)

Before I start packing, I decide how many of the clothing items I will need (three day trip = three pairs of socks, etc.) and I cross off any of the items that don't apply (if the hotel doesn't have a swimming pool, no need for swimming trunks). Then I go down the rest of the list, and packing takes only a few minutes. There may also be work tasks that you do repeatedly for which a list could be helpful. For instance, you might make a list of what needs to be included every time you write a press release.

BUSINESS LISTS

A great additional source of lists is the *Streetwise Small Business Book of Lists*, which features hundreds to help you reduce costs, increase revenue, and boost your profit. It's edited by Gene Marks and published by Adams Media.

Other times when a list could be useful include preparing for:

- Presentations.
- Networking events.
- Interviews.
- Negotiations.

Such lists can make it easier to delegate a task that you've been doing yourself, because the list will help ensure that the person taking it over doesn't forget or omit any important steps. Also make a list of the tasks you have delegated, indicating who is supposed to do it, by when, and with what outcome. You can then review this list every day and check in periodically with the people on the list to make sure they are on track to deliver as promised.

> *lists can make it easier to delegate a task that you've been doing yourself*

Another list to have handy is all the phone numbers of people you may need to contact when things go wrong. These could include a computer repair service, a software consultant, a temp agency, a delivery service, a store that delivers toner cartridges and other office supplies, and so on. Actually it's best to have at least two of each of these on your list. As we all know, things go awry at the most inconvenient points, when you don't want to lose more time by having to hunt around in a panic for the help you need.

What lists will help you focus?

Take a moment to think about three lists that might be helpful to you in your work, jot their names down here, and schedule time to make them.

_____

_____

_____

Do's and don't's for your to do list

The most common list that people use is the daily to do list. It's a great tool but often misused. It shouldn't be a dumping ground for every little thing you intend to get around to in the next few days or weeks. By all means, make up a master list of everything that needs your attention in the next week or so, but your daily list should contain only what you are committed to achieving that day. A good rule of thumb is to have a maximum of six items to focus on in one day.

If you find yourself repeatedly having to carry items over from one list to the next you are not being realistic about what you can achieve in the time available. The sense of daily failure will drain your energy. Put fewer items on the list. If you do have time to do more, go to your master list of things that need to be done and choose another task to work on.

If you like having things visible, you can also write each task on a sticky note, put it up on the wall, and take it down when you have accomplished it. Save the notes as a record of what you've achieved.

Keep those lists! Put your old to do lists in a folder or box and keep them for at least one year. If it ever becomes important for you to remember when you initiated a project or had a phone conversation, these lists will help.

In Chapter 10 you read about procrastination and your to do list and three ways to approach it. The ideal is to do the tasks in their order of importance, but since often the most important are also the most difficult, this can be hard. If you can't manage it, at least alternate between one easy and quick task and one more difficult but vital one in order to get rolling. Better yet, commit to doing the most important tasks first for just one week. By the end of the week the benefits will be so clear and energising that you'll find it a lot easier from then on.

Always carry a copy of your to do list with you. You can write or print out a mini-version of it on an index card that you keep in your pocket or bag. That way when you are in a meeting or out and about, you won't lose track of what else you still have to accomplish that day.

Finally, incorporate some time for relaxation and reflection in the list, even if it's only for a quarter of an hour once or twice a day. Treat this as seriously as any other task on the list – it shouldn't be the first item to be sacrificed if something else on the list takes longer than you thought. Remember that, in today's world, working smarter rather than harder is the road to success. Working smarter is the result of insights and creative thinking which require time and thought.

How to handle future tasks

There will be tasks that are important to do but that you know you don't need to do today. In fact, some of them, like certain phone calls or meetings, are tied to a future date. A great way to keep track of these is to make up a box with folders in it, numbered 1 to 31, one for each day of the month, plus 12 more with the names of the months on them. If today is 12th June, and you know that on the 20th you need to make a phone call to a potential client, you jot down a note to that effect and put it in the folder numbered 20. On the 19th, when you are planning what to do the next day, you open that folder and schedule the call. If the task doesn't need to be done until a day in August, you put it into the August folder. At the start of each month you check what's in the monthly folder and apportion it to a particular day-folder.

Now that you know how to handle paperwork much more efficiently, there remains one other subject that has become both a boon and a bane: email. In the next chapter, you'll find strategies for taming the email monster.

Website chapter bonus

At www.focusquick.com you'll find PDF forms to use with the filing system suggested in this chapter.

12

How to tame the email monster

Now that you have a good handle on how to deal with information overload and paperwork there's one more source of frustration that plagues just about everybody these days: email. On the one hand it's a brilliant way of communicating with people around the world almost instantly and it has revolutionised how we work. On the other, due to SPAM and the sheer number of even legitimate messages you get, it is also incredibly annoying and can easily pull you away from the things that should be taking up your time and attention. Not only that, sending emails can also be full of pitfalls. In this chapter you'll find the best strategies for making email the great tool it was always designed to be.

Control the clock

Unless you're responsible for, say, the defence of the Free World, do you really need to read every email the moment it comes in? Probably not. In that case, set a number of times each day that you will check your email. Do you have a number in mind? Good, now cut it in half. There are very few people who really need to do this more than four times a day, and three or two times a day is even better. For starters, try this schedule:

- When you get to your desk in the morning.
- Just after lunch.
- An hour before the end of the day.

If you have been in the habit of responding to emails immediately and are worried that people will wonder what's going on if you stop suddenly, you can turn on an automatic message, as you may do when you're going to be out of the office. It can say something like, "In order to increase my efficiency and therefore also my ability to help you, I'm now checking my emails at 9 am, 2 pm, and 5 pm. If you have something that needs my immediate attention, please give me a ring on (phone number)." That way people who do have an emergency won't feel upset, and generally a phone call is a better way of handling a super-urgent matter anyway. What you'll discover is that there are actually very few super-urgent matters.

Your new email schedule

If you have trouble sticking to set times, another approach is to check email only between tasks. If you do it during tasks, it will destroy your focus.

Jot down the times of day you are going to check email from now on. Also make a copy of these times and post them on or near your computer.

Email option one: deleting

The fastest way to deal with an email is to delete it. Obviously it's easy to do this with any SPAM that gets through. If too much is getting through, adjust or replace your SPAM filter. However, there are a lot of emails that seem like they might be interesting. These become a way of killing time instead of doing the 20% of your most valuable tasks. If you have been using them this way, consider using one of the Alter Egos you developed in Chapter 6 – Attila might be a good choice – and zap ruthlessly. Here are two big categories of email that are ripe for zapping:

- Jokes, weird news items, cartoons, etc. Most of these are probably coming from a small number of people. You have a choice: you can zap, or you can move to a "free-time" folder. You can also send an email back to the sender saying something along the lines of, "Although the jokes and cartoons you send me are good for a chuckle, I'm having trouble coping with the overload in my email inbox, so please don't send any more. I do appreciate the thought, and I'm sure you'll understand."

- Copies of emails sent to someone else, often marked "for your information". If you keep getting information you don't really need, these are just as bad as SPAM. Again, you have to train the people sending you these, with a gentle message like, "I appreciate your desire to keep me in the loop on this, but you don't actually need to copy me on these messages." Important: if there is a circumstance under which you *do* want to be notified, then you can add a qualifier, such as, "unless the project falls behind schedule", or "unless you need my direct participation".

Your deleting Alter Ego

Which of the Alter Egos you developed in Chapter 7 will you now use to zap irrelevant emails?

_____

Email option two: delegate

You've deleted, now delegate. If an email asks you to take some action, don't automatically do it. First consider whether it would be a better use of someone else's time (assuming, of course, that you have the authority to do this). If so, forward it to that person with a note saying what you want them to do. This could be as simple as, "Maria, please handle this", or it might require more detail. Then let the sender know that you've delegated it and that any further discussion of it should be taken up directly with Maria. The more you can eliminate yourself as the person in the middle, the better. This applies even to small things. For instance, sometimes I receive a message from one of my websites saying that one of

The man who doesn't understand SPAM.

I was going to order Viagra, but now that this Nigerian chap is going to send me £12 million, I'll be attracting women anyway!

JW

the links is dead or a particular video doesn't play correctly. My first impulse is to go to the site myself and check it – even though I have no idea of what to do if it is broken. Now I just pass the email along to my tech person and ask him to let me know when it's been fixed or to notify the sender if the problem is at their end.

"You've deleted, now delegate. "

If the person to whom you want to delegate is a colleague on the same level as you, rather than a subordinate, you'll have to handle it differently; namely, by going back to the sender and convincing them that Maria is the more appropriate person to handle this task. You may be tempted to handle it yourself, especially if it doesn't take too long, but when you do that you're also establishing the precedent that you're the one to come to whenever something similar needs to be handled in the future.

If there is no person handy who can deal with the task, and especially if you are self-employed, consider whether you could outsource it to a virtual assistant or via a relevant service.

Your delegation plan

Who can you think of, to whom you could delegate at least some of the email-related tasks that you do now?

Email option three: deal with it

For the remaining emails you can use a system of virtual folders identical to the real folders recommended in the previous chapters. Anything you need to handle today can go into a folder with the number of today's date, and then you can schedule it at the time of day that suits you best. Generally it's best to cluster these tasks rather than doing them piecemeal. If it can wait, then you can put it into a folder with another day's date and tackle it then. If it concerns something that will need your attention more than a month from now, you can put it into the folder for that month.

If you are handling several projects at once you may want to set up a separate system for each one. When you're planning your to do list for the following day, you can quickly go through the folders for that day and work out your schedule. An alternative, if you like to see things more openly than that is to have a separate calendar for each project and put the tasks onto the calendars.

You may already have another way of sorting and filing your emails that you prefer; that's fine, the main point is not to let them pile up into a wodge of a hundred or more that you keep having to review each time you open your inbox.

There are a couple of types of emails that are particularly troublesome:

The never-ending message

> "The art of art, the glory of expression and the sunshine of light of letters, is simplicity."
> Walt Whitman, Poet (1819–1892)

There's a great quote that has been attributed to many people, including Mark Twain and Abraham Lincoln. It's a postscript to a long missive that read, "I'm sorry I wrote such a long letter. I didn't have time to write a short one." You probably know people who write long, long emails that would be much better if they were shorter. If you're in a position to do so, you can suggest to them that they start the email with a very short summary of the key points. If they're in the habit of sending you emails that include a long string of previous email exchanges, ask them just to summarise what has gone before. If the originator of these endless emails is your boss you may have to suffer through them. But you can use the same techniques as you would to skim printed material: start by reading the first and last paragraphs, and the first sentence of each paragraph. Often that's enough to give you the gist of the message.

The emails someone should never have sent

You may find yourself on the receiving end of an emotional email, something that obviously was written in the heat of the moment, or after the sender had a long, liquid lunch. If you're the merciful type the best course of action is to pretend you never received it, or let a few hours or a day go by and then email the person back, saying your inbox showed there was an email from them but you couldn't open it. They may see right through this ruse but they'll be eternally grateful nonetheless.

The do's and don't's of sending emails

The easiest way to know what to do when sending emails is to think about all the things that others do that really annoy you or waste your time, and then don't do those. Here are a few specific methods that will make people appreciate getting emails from you:

Use the subject line to give information

If the gist of your message is that you want someone to go ahead with a purchase that was discussed that morning, don't make the subject line, "Re: purchasing new printer" and then write more in the body of the message. In the subject line just write, "Please go ahead and purchase the printer we discussed this A.M." and leave the body of the message blank. It will save time and set an admirable example of brevity.

Don't use emails for sensitive messages

If you have to tell someone their work is not up to snuff, or, even worse, that they're fired, that's not an appropriate message for an email. Go and talk to the person or at the very least use the phone. And never use emails to pass along any gossip or rumours. Emails can be printed out easily and often are. If you don't want a permanent record of what you said making its way around the office, don't email it. We read all the time about people who were foolish about what they said in emails and how it cost them their jobs or their relationships. For some reason, we think it can't possibly happen to us. That's what they used to think, too.

Don't use emails to admit your mistakes

Again, this is sensitive stuff that is best handled in a meeting. One of the drawbacks of email is that it does not convey any emotional nuances, not even if you use smiley and frowny faces. Any message with emotional content of any kind is best dealt with another way.

Start your email with a brief statement that makes it clear what it's about

An email that starts, "No, it's not a good idea" and then goes on for a while about why it's not a good idea is not very helpful if the reader doesn't know what "it" is. Remember that your email may appear in the middle of 50 or 100 others, so don't expect the recipient to remember what "it" was, and don't make them go down to the bottom of the email to re-read their original message to you. Ideally your subject line has already told them this is about "Revamping the reception area" – even better, it told them, "Revamping reception – I don't agree." Then, if necessary, the body of the message can set out your three reasons for not agreeing.

Don't forget the attachments

We've all been there: we write an email promising an attachment, forget to attach it, have to write an "oops" email, this time with the attachment. Simple solution: get into the habit of attaching the file before you write the message.

Be very specific about what you expect the recipient to do

If you're sending an email requesting that the other person take action, be as clear as possible regarding what you want them to do, including deadlines if appropriate.

If you are addressing several projects, send one email per project

It will be a lot easier for the recipient to file your messages in appropriate folders.

Treat emails with as much dignity and respect as you would any written message

There's no reason to use colourful backgrounds, or emoticons or incorrect grammar or punctuation in business messages. Your emails send a secondary message about you and your image.

The bottom line: stay in charge

Here's the key message of this chapter: control email rather than letting it control you. It's there to serve you, not to frustrate or annoy you. You can choose whether and when to read it. You can choose whether and when to answer it. You can even train people regarding what to send you, and the best manner in which to send it. And when you send email to others, you can model these effective behaviours so that both you and the recipient benefit. All this will prevent email from distracting you from your most important tasks.

Now that you know how to handle email without stress, the next chapter provides tools for mastering meetings and networking.

Website chapter bonus

At www.focusquick.com you'll find a short video about using Alter Egos to handle email.

13

How to master meetings and networking

Other than information overload, paperwork, and emails, the two topics that cause the most anxiety and frustration at work are meetings and networking. In this chapter you'll find techniques for handling both. Let's start with meetings and the most important questions you must ask.

Is this meeting really necessary?

Deleting is an important technique for handling paperwork and emails, and it applies just as much to meetings. Once they get started, meetings seem to take on a (long) life of their own. We'll see in a moment how to minimise that, but even better is to cut out as many meetings as possible. If you are the one deciding whether to call a meeting, consider whether a memo, email, phone call, or brief conference call could achieve just as much.

Is your presence really required?

If the meeting is called by someone else, consider whether it's actually relevant to you. If not, don't go. If you need to justify this to someone above you, make your case concisely, stressing how much more value it would provide if you took this time to work on your most important tasks.

If you're needed for only one of the items on the agenda, see whether you can get that one scheduled first so you can leave once it has been handled. If not, and the meeting is going to be a long one, offer to pop in quickly when someone pages or phones you to let you know that your item is up next.

Do you all know the purpose of the meeting?

A lot of meetings run on and on because there is no clear agenda. The purpose is stated in vague terms like, "to review progress on the Martin project" or "to catch up on whatever issues may have come up in the past month". This is a recipe for a rambling, unfocused session that wastes time on the unimportant 80%. Somebody needs to create a precise agenda that should be circulated in advance. If this is missing from your meetings, make the case for an agenda to your boss or, if you are the boss, arrange for it yourself.

Is everybody prepared?

If you expect participants to have specific information to share, that should also go on the agenda or a memo that goes with it. That way nobody can claim surprise that they were supposed to be ready with facts and figures to move the discussion forward.

Is there a schedule and time limit?

If a warm-up chat seems like a necessary part of the meeting in order to get everybody's minds off whatever they were doing a few minutes ago, set a time limit for it. You can go around the room and every person gets a couple of minutes to mention how they're getting on. If anybody runs over their time and shows no signs of stopping, the chairperson has to move things along.

TIPS FOR FAST MEETINGS

- When possible, have people come to your location.
- Keep the room temperature cool to keep people alert.
- For one-to-ones have the meeting while taking a walk.

Ideally a time limit for discussion of each item will be noted on the agenda. It can be enforced by a timer that signals that the time for this item is about to run out. If it becomes clear that any item will require a great deal more time, it's better to schedule a separate additional meeting for it rather than let it derail all the other items. Naturally this also means that there will be a time limit for the meeting as a whole. Just as work expands to fill the time available, so do meetings. Knowing that limits will be enforced concentrates everybody's mind and they will say what needs saying in much less time.

One clever strategy is to schedule a one-hour meeting one hour before lunch or quitting time. Everyone will be anxious to stay on schedule.

"schedule a one-hour meeting one hour before lunch"

Are the decisions made in the meeting clear?

Naturally someone should be recording the decisions reached during the meeting and who has agreed to what future action. At the end of each agenda item the person doing this recording can summarise these points in one or two sentences. These items can then also go into a summary memo that will be distributed to the participants and to anybody else who needs to know this information. This will prevent those, "Oh, I thought we agreed to something different!" problems.

If it's a brainstorming meeting are you following the four guidelines?

If the meeting is designed to yield new ideas, follow the four guidelines of brainstorming:

1 Quantity is king. The idea of a brainstorming session is to generate as many ideas as possible.

Is this the meeting, or
the meeting about the meeting?

2 No judging. Judging ideas at the same time you're coming up with them stops the flow. Later there will be a time for evaluation.

3 Write everything down. Writing down some things and not others is a form of judging. Be sure there are enough big flip charts or sheets of paper or white boards around to be able to write everything down in big letters.

4 Don't be afraid to build on someone else's idea. Sometimes a little refinement really improves a concept.

Are you keeping the meeting as simple as possible?

When possible, stick to flip charts or white boards and pens. Avoid PowerPoint or anything else that requires technical equipment. It breaks down. We've all been in meetings where suddenly the projector's bulb burns out, or the laptop connection doesn't fit, or the computer freezes up. It's embarrassing and a waste of time.

> "Meetings are indispensable when you don't want to do anything."
>
> John Kenneth Galbraith, Economist (1908–2006)

Have the ground rules been set?

There are a few ground rules that will help make meetings more productive and pleasant. Already alluded to above is the expectation that everyone will come to the meeting prepared. Here are a few additional expectations:

- Everyone will be on time. Drastic but effective: lock out any late-comers. Next time they'll be on time.

- Mobile phones and Blackberries will be turned off. Drastic but effective: confiscate them at the door. You can make a lighthearted "Hand over your guns at the saloon door" allusion, but participants will get the point.

- Everyone will be expected to stay awake. Drastic but effective (also good for keeping meetings briefer): take the chairs out of the room so everyone stands up for the duration of the meeting.

- While spirited discussion is fine, there will be basic respect for each other, as evidenced by not interrupting others and not dominating the conversation. If necessary, this should be enforced by the chairperson.

- During lengthy meetings there will be reasonable toilet breaks.

- There will be healthy snacks (especially fruit) and water available.

You may not be able to control or influence all the elements of a meeting, but changing even a few of them can make a big difference. If you're not in a decision-making position regarding how and when meetings are conducted, discuss it with the people who are – it's likely they are just as frustrated as you with overly-long and unfocused meetings and will welcome your ideas.

Which of the above strategies can you implement or suggest in order to make a difference in the meetings in which you take part?

_____

_____

The networking nemesis

One type of meeting that deserves its own section is networking. Here's a little test. The following is an actual quote from an entrepreneur who shall remain nameless. Read it and notice how it makes you feel: "[Networking] is so fun and fulfilling ... Talk to people all the time, in line at the store, at the salon, on an airplane ... Not sure how to start? Offer a compliment. There's always something attractive or admirable to notice about a stranger. Be sincere about it."

If you're thinking, "Of course, that's absolutely right!" skip the rest of this chapter because you're obviously (a) American and (b) a natural-born networker. However, if it makes you feel slightly queasy, stick with me, we're going to explore alternatives that allow you to focus on your strengths – even if networking isn't one of them.

The normal networking event tends to consist of a lot of people thrusting business cards at each other while trying to balance a glass of wine. At the end of the evening, you have a pocket or purse full of business cards and you don't remember who any of them belonged to. All the people who have *your* business cards feel the same. The usual advice is for you to show interest in the other person. This results in two people both pretending to be interested in the other person but secretly waiting to talk about themselves and whatever they're offering. My advice: if you're not comfortable going to these kinds of networking events, don't go. Yes, it's important to make contacts, but there are other ways. We'll get to those in a moment, but if you do find yourself at a networking event, there are some guidelines that will make it more productive.

Find your most effective networking Alter Ego

Are there times when you do enjoy meeting new people? Times when you are relaxed and confident in presenting yourself? Either remember such a time, or imagine what that would be like, and create an Alter Ego for that state. Get into that state whenever you choose to go to a networking event. Don't necessarily try to model those enthusiastic, outgoing, thrusting-handshake people who are often presented as ideal networkers; rather, find a version with which you will feel comfortable.

Go to the 20% of events most likely to pay off

There are so many conventions, meetings, business parties and other events going on all the time that it's important to priori-tise and go only to the 20% that are likely to give you 80% of your pay-offs. These events have two elements in common:

- Most of the people there will not be in the same line of business as you. What's the point of going to a meeting of insurance agents if you're one yourself? Sure, it can be fun to talk shop and complain about certain types of clients or the latest government red tape, but it's not going to get you more business. Going to some event where you'll find the kind of people likely to need the sort of insurance you sell would be much more promising.

- There is something going on other than networking. It might be an awards ceremony, a celebration of some kind, or a charity event. This gives you something to talk about other than yourself. If people are interested in what you do, you can mention it briefly and, if they're still interested, they may ask you for your card. But none of it will feel awkward or like a hard sell. If you can't afford the price of admission, volunteer to register guests or help with refreshments. Just be sure you'll also have a bit of time to circulate.

What kinds of events could you go to that fulfil the above criteria?

_____

_____

How to make schmoozing painless

Arrive at social functions early and chat with as many people as possible. Again, you don't have to do a hard sell. Those who are potential customers will naturally be interested in what you do.

A good way to let people know what you do is to ask them what they do. Give them the same quality of attention you hope to receive – after all, you're also a potential customer for them.

You don't need an opening line to start a conversation. Just comment on whatever is happening. If a lighthearted comment comes to mind, so much the better, but any kind of statement can get the ball rolling: "What did you think of the speaker?" or "This is a good turnout, isn't it?" However, be ready with a statement of more substance or a question once the ice is broken.

Are you shy? Scan the room for other shy people to talk to. They will be grateful that someone is talking to them. But don't get stuck talking to the same person all night.

For a hosted event establish an easy escape path if you're not enjoying it or it's not serving your needs. If you warn your host that you may need to leave early you can cut the evening short without offending anybody.

How to be a hermit and still network

There's now a great alternative to networking in person: the internet. If you're not into small talk over cocktails, you can still meet people, at least virtually. Find out which websites are most popular with the kind of people that you want to attract to your business, and hang out there. Leave comments on blogs and website forums, making them relevant and helpful, with only minimal reference to your own site and business. When you become a regular on these sites, people will start asking you about what you do. Then you can give more details.

If you're the shy type, why not get people to come to you? Wouldn't it be great not to have to deal with the 80% of people who are not in the market for your services, and attract the 20% who are? As a lure, you should have a website of your own, with articles and tips regarding your subject, and a way for people to contact you.

A blog can be even better, because it's easier to add to than a website, and you can use it to build up a fan base. Encourage people to leave comments but don't despair if they don't. Don't expect results right away, it takes a while for people to find you. Once you have a substantial number of posts and, ideally, some other blogs and websites linking to you, the search engines will begin to lead people to you as well. Don't go for the hard sell on a blog, just let people get to know you.

If you let your blog (or podcast, or site) reflect your personality, people will get a sense of what it would be like to work with you, and business will appear. Decide how often you want to post new items, and stick to that.

> "Never fear the want of business. A many who qualifies himself well for his calling, never fails of employment."
> *Thomas Jefferson (1743–1826)*

You can also write articles about your topic and post them to websites like www.ezinearticles.com. Each article will carry a bio and links to your site at the end. These articles are read and also may then be picked up by other sites. For example, as I write, I have 23 writing-related articles on that site and they have been read 2500 times and picked up by a total of 190 ezine publishers. The effects are slow and long-term, and this works best if you continue to contribute articles on a regular basis.

Consider writing an article for a local publication about some aspect of what you do. The editor will allow you to add your name, the name of your business, and contact information at the end. If you have specialist knowledge that could be of general interest, you may be able to write a regular column. Other outlets include company newsletters and trade publications.

If it's appropriate to what you do, consider publishing a quarterly newsletter. Even if the primary purpose is advertising your products or services, make sure it has enough valuable information in it to make it worth reading.

Are you more comfortable speaking rather than writing? Consider creating a podcast. As with posts on a blog, how often you create new episodes is not as important as developing a regular schedule. And if you're happy to do some public speaking, that's another great way to get people to come to you.

Which of the above methods of attracting people to yourself and your work do you think would be most productive for you?

_____

_____

In this chapter, we've covered ways to add focus to meetings and networking, so they become relatively painless and more likely to lead to the results you want. You can add these to the considerable arsenal you've gained in all the previous chapters. How to apply all of these tools so you easily meet your deadlines even when juggling several projects is the topic of the next chapter.

Website chapter bonus

At www.focusquick.com you will find a short film that shows the rights and wrongs of meetings.

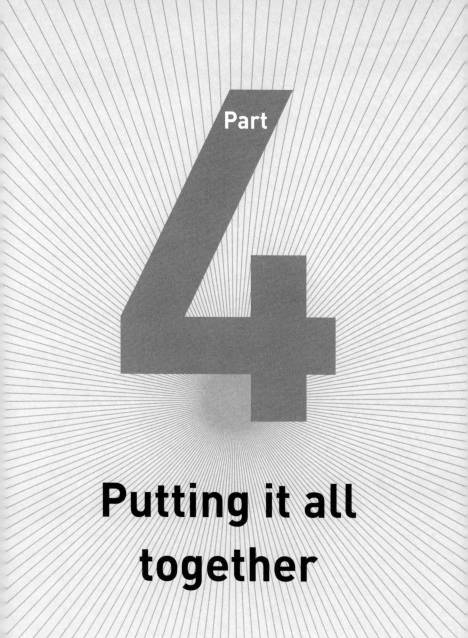

Part

4

Putting it all together

14

CHAPTER FOURTEEN

How to deal with deadlines and multiple projects

When you have only one project to work on, maintaining focus is a lot easier than when you are juggling several. However, doing just one project at a time is a luxury for most people. In this chapter you'll find out how to manage adroitly several projects at the same time. You'll also learn the best techniques for making sure you meet your deadlines.

How to set deadlines by working backward

There's an old question that is sometimes asked regarding deadlines: "Do you want it good, or do you want it fast?" In today's marketplace the answer is "Both!" If you put into action the strategies we've already covered, you'll be most of the way there to delivering both. The first step is to be sure that the deadline to which you agree is reasonable.

The best way to set deadlines is to work backward from the goal. Begin with the final step and then indicate the step you need to take just before that one, then the one just before that one, and so on. Let's say that you are going to organise and present a one-day workshop scheduled for 15 July. Here's part of the working-backward list:

- 15 July: The workshop itself.

- 14 July: Final email to all participants confirming times, location, etc/Final check that audio-visual equipment will be in place/Final confirmation with catering department re coffee and biscuits for breaks.

- 12 July: Photocopy all the handouts needed for the workshop.

- 10 July: Double-check that requested audio-visual equipment has been ordered.

- 8 July: Place order for refreshments with catering department.

Just about any kind of project can be broken down into these kinds of steps. With a long-term project that involves people not under your direct control you may not be able to attach exact dates to every step. Even so, it's useful to attach target dates to help you track your progress. Be sure to build in some extra time in every phase of the project. Too many people schedule a project on the assumption that everything will go to plan, regardless of the fact that every day proves the opposite. Somewhere along the line, someone will get the 'flu and be out for a week, a supplier will go out of business and leave you in the lurch, and a print job will come back with a big mistake and need to be redone. Build in time for human and technological error. If, by some miracle, nothing goes wrong and you reach the goal early – congratulations!

A working backward visualisation

A visualisation can help you work backward from your goal. For an example let's use the goal of having a national talk show (a fairly common goal these days, it seems ...). When you do the visualisation naturally you'll substitute a goal that is meaningful for you.

Allocate about 15 minutes for this exercise. Close your eyes, relax, take the first minute or two to breathe slowly and deeply. Then see, hear, and feel what things will be like when you have achieved the goal. This is really another version of the Alter Ego strategy – in this case, you are assuming the identity of the version of you that has already reached the goal.

Take your time and enjoy it. Here are the kinds of things to attend to:

- What are people saying to you? What kinds of questions are they asking?

- What are your surroundings? Who is there with you?

- How does it make you feel?

Staying in that reverie, now imagine yourself being interviewed for a magazine article. The interviewer is interested in how you got where you are today. In your imagination, hear their questions and your answers. Don't force the answers, just let them come up.

Let the interviewer be probing but not threatening. For example, if they ask, "How did you get to be the host of this national talk show?" maybe your answer is, "Well, I did a local talk show first, and that was so successful that I was asked to do this one." Perhaps next they ask, "What made that local show so special?" and then "How did that local show come to be?"

Give yourself time – the advantage of imaginary interviews is that you can take all the time you want to let an answer emerge. Don't judge your answers, just play along.

When the interview is finished, come back out of the daydream, out of that Alter Ego, and jot down everything you remember. Some people prefer to have a tape recorder going while they're daydreaming and describe what's happening as they go along.

Put the notes away and come back to them another day. Underline all those things that refer to the steps you saw leading up to your goal. Use a clean sheet of paper to put them in rough chronological order, from now to the achievement of your goal. If for some you don't know what the order should be, guess.

Pick a step that strikes you as possibly being halfway to your goal. In our example, it might be the point at which you're just starting your local TV show. Repeat the process: take 20 minutes to daydream about how that looks, sounds, and feels. Assume the Alter Ego of the you that has reached that point. Then take part in another interview. Jot down your findings, pick out steps, and put them in order. Each time you do this, you will get a greater level of detail.

> If you'd prefer to be led through this visualisation, at the www.focusquick.com website you will find instructions for how to purchase this and other visualisations.

Depending on how ambitious a goal you've chosen, you may need to do this another time or two (each time cutting the remaining distance in half), before you realise that you've come up with a series of steps that are quite comfortable for you to start on right now. In our example, that might be joining a class in public speaking or it might be getting a video camera and taping yourself so you can begin to master the various skills required by a talk show host.

All of the information can be used for creating your goal maps which will guide you through all the steps. One of the challenges of implementation is allocating the correct amount of time for the tasks you have to accomplish along the way.

Use your time-estimating history

Based on your experience with other projects, which of these is most accurate regarding how well you estimate how long things will take?

❏ "I usually underestimate by 50% or more."

❏ "I usually underestimate by about 25% to 50%."

❏ "I usually underestimate by about 10% to 25%."

❏ "I usually estimate very close to the actual time it takes."

❏ "I usually overestimate by about 10% to 25%."

❏ "I usually overestimate by 25% or more."

How you answer this question will give you a rough guide to how to adjust your estimates of how much time to allocate for completion of your next project. If you routinely underestimate by 25%, next time add at least 25% more time to your estimate. If you want to be more certain of coming in on time, add another 10% on top of that. It's much better to surprise clients by completing a project early than to surprise them by missing the declared deadline.

Remember the three D's

At every step of the way, decide which of our three D's apply: Delete, Delegate, or Do. If you can safely skip a step, do so. If someone else can do it faster, better, or more cheaply than you, if it's not in the 20% of your 80/20 analysis, delegate it. Otherwise, do it. The most successful people automatically review these options every step of the way.

Your visualisation, as well as any previous experience you've had with similar projects, will have alerted you to potential obstacles. Spend some extra time planning how to overcome them. Ideally you will pre-identify two or more options for how to handle potential trouble spots.

❝Your visualisation, will have alerted you to potential obstacles. ❞

Monitor your progress

It will be easy to monitor your own progress using your goal maps. If you are depending on others to deliver elements of the project you will have to monitor their progress as well. If their tasks are long term or substantial, agree upon milestones that you can check so that there are no unpleasant surprises when they reach their deadlines.

Let me tell you a story about how this can go wrong. I once hired a freelance writer to prepare a series of case studies that would be integrated with a major report that my company was preparing for the government. Every week I checked in with her and she assured me that she was making good progress. When it was time for her to submit her work, not only did she not show up, she stopped answering her phone. Finally I reached her husband, who informed me that she was suffering from mental strain and had only imagined doing the work. Why he didn't think this might be something to share with me earlier in the process is another question, but the upshot was that a week before the report was due, there were no case studies. It took me a week of 18-hour days to create them. That was how I learned to observe the maxim, "Don't expect – *inspect!*"

What are three ways you can begin to apply the "Don't expect – inspect!" principle in your work?

_____

_____

_____

AVOID THE BLAME GAME!

When something goes wrong it's easy to focus on whose fault it is instead of on solutions. It's more constructive to ask these three questions:

1. What can be done now to solve the problem?
2. Who is the best person to solve it?
3. What can we do to prevent this problem from happening again?

Be alert to implications and opportunities

When one part of the plan goes wrong, it can have implications for steps further down the line. Review each goal map frequently and revise it as necessary. If you have built in sufficient time for hitches, they should not affect your overall timeline very much. If something big comes up figure out what other elements of your plan will be affected and what you need to do about it. It may be that you have to bring in extra help, trim some of the deliverables, or otherwise modify the original to stay on schedule. If you do need to adjust the delivery date, notify anybody else who is affected as early as possible.

It's equally possible that along the way you will find ways to shortcut a part of the process, perhaps by using new technology or figuring out how to delegate more than you originally thought possible. All too often, people get so attached to their plans that they don't recognise such opportunities. While your goal may not change, the best way to get there should remain open to change at all times.

Keep your outdated project maps and review them periodically to see whether the adjustments you've made suggest anything to do differently during the rest of the project or lessons you can apply to future projects.

Isolate the problems

If you find yourself falling behind, don't just try to do everything a bit faster. Isolate the problem: what is causing you to miss your targets? Is it someone else who is not delivering? If that's the case, here are the most important questions to consider:

- Do they understand what you expect of them? If not, how will you alter the way you communicate with them to make this clearer? One option is to give them a copy of the goal map so they can understand fully how their work affects the rest of the tasks.

- Have they agreed to deliver what you expect of them, when you expect it?

- Have you established milestones to make sure that they progress at the agreed upon pace? Do you have an inspection method in place?

- If they are not delivering, what is the problem? What do you and they need to do to make sure the problem is solved?

- What backup do you have in place in case this solution doesn't work?

If you are the source of the problem, ask yourself these questions:

- What's the specific reason that you're falling behind?

- What can you do immediately to remedy the situation? This may require you to take a step back from the situation and see it from a different perspective. As Einstein pointed out, you can't solve a problem at the same level at which it was created. By looking at it from the viewpoint of several Alter Egos, the technique described in Chapter 7, you will gain a lot more information about what's really happening.

- If you are still having a hard time figuring out the problem or the solution, who can help? Ideally this is someone who can take a fresh, unbiased look at the situation and give you constructive feedback. Just hearing someone else's view can be enough to prompt new ideas for solutions.

- Can you implement the solution without negatively affecting your other obligations? Stealing time or other resources from one project to serve another will only shift the problem, not solve it.

Build momentum with a MAD

In most projects there are points where progress has slowed down, or delays or other hiccups have caused a loss not only of momentum but perhaps also of morale. These are the perfect time for an ultra-focusing technique I refer to as a

MAD: Massive Action Day. This is a day when you put aside everything else and give your total focus to achieving as much in those 8 or 10 or 12 hours as you might ordinarily expect to accomplish in a week. Naturally this is not a pace you would expect to keep up all the time; it's the equivalent of a long-distance runner putting on a sprint at some point to pass a competitor. It can inject new energy into a project and revive your and other people's enthusiasm and confidence. Here's how to conduct a MAD:

- Get all necessary supplies and documents together the day before. On your MAD you don't want to waste a single moment looking for files or staples or anything else.

- Set out clear goals for that day right at the beginning. Work out an hour-by-hour schedule to aim for. Check off all tasks as you finish them, to keep up the feeling of a flow of accomplishment.

- Schedule short breaks every 90 minutes. Research suggests that 90 minutes is the period in which we have a cycle of attention, so taking a 10-minute break every hour and a half will be more productive than working through.

- Do something physical during your breaks: a quick walk around the building or up and down the stairs, stretches, even running in place are all fine. Anything that gets the blood flowing.

- Have lots of water and healthy snacks available. If you use coffee or tea to stay alert, have it in small quantities throughout the day, not in big servings at only a few points.

- Do something to celebrate and reward yourself at the end of a MAD – have a good dinner, or watch a film, or whatever works for you.

Is there a task or project in your life now that is stalled and would benefit from a MAD? If so, describe it here and indicate when you will have a MAD to get it rolling again:

_____

Another secret weapon for focus: the Time Capsule

It's not practical to have a MAD too often, but you can use another technique to get optimal results within a much shorter time period. I call this one the Time Capsule, and I suggest you apply it to 90-minute chunks of time. Here's how it works:

- Get a sheet of paper. At the top, write what you will achieve in the next 90 minutes. Be ambitious.

- Below that write down everything you will need in order to reach the goal, such as certain files, office supplies, books, etc.

- Assemble everything you listed as necessary.

- Turn off your phone, put a "Do not disturb" sign on your desk, and do whatever else is necessary to ensure you will not be interrupted. If necessary, go to a different location.

- Set a timer (such as a kitchen timer, or one that appears on your computer desktop, or even an alarm clock) to go off in 90 minutes.

- Go to work. Don't interrupt yourself by checking for emails or phone messages, or anything else. Just do it.

- If you finish before the alarm goes off, go on to the next step. Otherwise, stop when the alarm rings.

- At the bottom of the sheet, jot down anything useful you've learned about what you achieved (or didn't) in this

Time Capsule. For instance, if you found you were distracted by the noise coming from the next cubicle, that may be a good indicator that for your next Time Capsule you need to relocate.

If you didn't achieve everything you hoped to in that 90 minutes, you have the option of moving the undone portion into another Time Capsule. But first take a short break, do anything necessary that might otherwise distract you, and then repeat the process. It's very important that you actually do the writing down part of the process. That's what helps you to really focus and to learn from what works and doesn't work so that you become more skilful each time you use a Time Capsule. You can download a PDF of a Time Capsule form from the www.focusquick.com website and photocopy it.

How to panic

If you use all of these methods you should never find it necessary to panic. If a project does go off the rails despite your best efforts and requires a major effort for you to make the deadline, there are some constructive ways to shape your panic so it works for you instead of against you. As you'll see, some of these are an extension of the methods you use in a MAD:

- Be ruthless in eliminating everything within the project that is not absolutely necessary. This is the time to trim any elements that may be considered extras. Now your goal is to deliver only the things you absolutely promised. If you have any vestiges of perfectionism, lose them. Until you get back on track, your new target is "good enough".

- Be equally ruthless in eliminating everything outside of the project that is not absolutely necessary. If this project hinges on you putting in more time, cancel all social occasions and defer other projects if you can do so without fatal consequences for them. Get only enough exercise and sleep to keep you alert and working well.

- Get help. Delegating even a few basic elements, such as proofreading, fact-checking, and even going out to keep your coffee supply constant can help. If the project is a team effort, create an "all hands on deck" atmosphere. Pizza, music, and even some brief goofy games to keep everybody alert can help. Promise some rewards to those who are willing to make the same sacrifices you are. For example, if you're asking people to work late, let them know that they'll get generous compensatory time off when the panic is over.

These are extraordinary measures and should be reserved for exceptional times. If every project you do ends up in this kind of panic, you're failing to plan. When the panic is over, take some time to analyse what you could have done differently to avoid it and how you will do those things next time around.

Jones is our expert in how to panic.

How to manage multiple projects

Few people have the luxury of working on only one project at a time. Indeed, many creative people get bored if they do. Whether by choice or by demand, it's likely you have to juggle several projects at the same time. More often than you might think, it's possible to leverage this to your advantage. To make that work, there are a few things you need to do:

- As mentioned previously, make a goal map for each of the projects, with indications of when you hope to achieve each step. That way you can align them to see the collection of tasks you need to do in a given week and on a given day.

- Bunch similar activities and schedule yourself by activity rather than by project. If for two projects you need to do some research on the internet and to make some phone calls, you'll work more efficiently if you do all the research and then make all the phone calls, rather than researching Project A, making the phone calls for Project A, then switching back to researching for Project B and then calls for Project B.

- Whatever you are learning or experiencing for one project, actively look for ways that you can apply it to your other active projects. This doesn't require that the projects be similar; in fact, often the most creative solutions come about when someone takes something that works in one context and applies it in another. For instance, the lessons of uniformity of processes that were developed by McDonald's have now been applied to lots of other businesses.

- Use your down time on one project to make progress on another one. When you reach a point where you can't advance a project, perhaps because you're waiting for input from someone else, it's tempting to switch to some of your 80% low-value activity. If it's time for a break, by all means take one, but otherwise this is a great time to look at your other goal maps and see what you can accomplish while waiting. Notice that this is *not* multitasking, which has been widely discredited. It turns out, maybe not too surprisingly, that when we try to do two things at once, we don't do either of them as well as when we give our full attention to each.

How to time multiple projects

If you have a choice in the matter, it's ideal to stagger projects so that they don't have deadlines too close to each other. Despite your planning, you may find that the week or two before the deadline requires additional effort on your part. If that happens with two or more projects simultaneously it's a prescription for stress. Also, many people find that they prefer to have projects in different stages of activity, so that in a given week they may be in the planning phase of Project A, the early implementation of Project B, and finishing up Project C.

Another way to align projects is to arrange them so that the times when you will be delegating much of your work on one are the times that require your intensive involvement in another.

With these tools for reaching deadlines on target and applying your skills to multiple projects, you now have a complete suite of success techniques. Of course true success comes when all parts of your life are in balance, and that is the topic of the next chapter.

Website chapter bonus

At www.focusquick.com you will find downloadable PDF forms to use for Time Capsules. You may photocopy as many of these as you like.

15

CHAPTER FIFTEEN
How to maintain your new found focus

You now have a wealth of tools that will help you reach the goals you set, and in record time. In this chapter you'll find useful techniques for maintaining your new-found focus. As you'll discover, these include having a balanced life, allocating enough time for rest, exercise, and recreation, and maintaining a playful and creative attitude to life and work. These are the secrets of the truly successful people who work to live, not live to work.

Is your life balanced?

At the outset, you saw how the 80/20 principle can be applied in order to bring you the results you want in all areas of your life. However, our world tends to define success in very narrow terms, mostly involving money and the appearance of glamour. This, despite the fact that most people who attain fame and fortune say it comes at a heavy price. That's why many people end up putting all of their efforts into career or business success and forget that they also have the tools with which to create a great family and personal life.

If finding a balance may be a problem for you, come up with some goals for all the areas of your life and make sure that all of them are getting a fair share of your time and attention. These areas include:

- Health and fitness. Usually we take good health for granted – until we don't have it anymore. It's difficult to enjoy the other parts of your life fully if you're ill. Creating some goals for yourself around exercise, healthy eating, and rest and recreation makes sense.

- Family relationships. If you miss your children's early years because you're working too hard, will the gain be worth the sacrifice? Even if you think you've struck a good balance in this area, ask the experts: your spouse or partner, your children, and other members of your family. If their answer is different from yours, it may be time to reconsider how you're apportioning your time and energy.

- Friendships. Are you taking the time to stay in touch with old friends and make some new ones, especially with people outside the orbit of your work? Sometimes it's easy to think you'll do those kinds of things "later". If so, when will "later" be?

- Your religious or spiritual dimension. Only you know what form you'd like this to take, but are you giving it your attention?

- Community involvement. This can also take many different incarnations, from volunteer work to donations to your favourite charities, to just getting to know the neighbours.

Your non-work goals

Jot down at least one goal for each of these areas:

"The best and safest thing is to keep a balance in your life, acknowledge the great powers around us and in us. If you can do that, and live that way, you really are a wise man."
Euripides (484BC–406BC)

Health and fitness: _____

Family: _____

Friends: _____

Religious/spiritual: _____

Community: _____

Cutting back on sleep or exercise: a false economy

Some people are so driven or just so enthusiastic that they think getting less sleep is a good way to free up more time for pursuing their goals. Unfortunately, it doesn't take long for sleep deprivation to kick in. You may not even notice it at first, especially if you're trying to make up for it with increased doses of caffeine, but without enough rest your brain's ability to function quickly deteriorates. The effects include reduced concentration, loss of memory, irritability, and slower reaction times. Over time, it can even contribute to heart disease, hypertension, and tremors. Recent research also suggests that a lack of sleep may promote obesity.

Experts agree that the individual's need for sleep generally is between seven and eight hours a night. If you are getting less than that and often feel a low-grade tiredness, sleep deprivation may be the cause. Furthermore, it may be inhibiting your ability to come up with creative ideas. Experiment by adding some sleep time and you will be able to figure out how much you really need.

If you need to make a change in your sleep habits, summarise it here:

Similarly, some people say they are too busy to exercise – this, at a time when 60% of people in the UK and the US are overweight or obese, which we know can have grave implications for health (pun intended). This isn't a fitness book, but it is obvious that anyone who is not in good physical shape is going to have a harder time focusing and working effectively. If you are worried about wasting time, listen to podcasts or business-related audio books so you learn while you exercise.

If you need to make a change in your fitness habits, summarise it here:

The stress epidemic

Some of the phenomena we have already discussed, such as information overload and the belief that you have to be connected 24/7, greatly increase your stress levels, again with negative ramifications for your health. Adequate sleep, exercise, and some down time can all help counteract the stress epidemic. So can holidays and even mini-breaks that take you away from your normal routines for just half a day, ideally in a natural environment (if only your local park).

Can't spare even half a day right now? Start with smaller chunks of time when you pause to think about ... nothing at all. Sit at a sidewalk café, have a juice (not a double espresso), turn off your phone, and watch people go by. Notice how many of them are on mobile phones. Count the number who are smiling vs. the number who are frowning. Count the number who ever look up from the pavement to look at each other or their surroundings. Breathe deeply.

❝pause to think about . . . nothing at all❞

If you need to do more to de-stress, jot down one thing you will do today or tomorrow:

"The creation of something new is not accomplished by the intellect but by the play instinct acting from inner necessity."
Carl Jung (1875–1961)

Take time to play

The final suggestion in this chapter: find time to play. Playfulness and creativity are very closely connected, and it's working smart, not just working hard, that's going to account for your success. Some people have been working so hard for so long that they can't even think of anything silly or playful to do. For those, here is 30 days' worth of liberating foolishness (if this month has 31 days, you'll have to come up with one more idea yourself).

30 days of creativity

1. Write a country and western song about your life.
2. Ask your grandmother (in your imagination, if she's dead) what she would do about your most pressing problem.

3. Read your own tea leaves. Write down whatever comes to mind as you peer at the dregs.

4. If you were a famous brand, what would your slogan be? What would you like it to be? What do you have to do to justify the one you'd like?

5. Go to a park for an hour in the middle of the day and people watch.

6. Make three genuine compliments to the people you meet today. Notice their reactions.

7. Go to an art gallery for half an hour. Pick one painting to study for at least 10 minutes.

8. Make up a bedtime story for yourself before you go to sleep.

9. Send a friend a thank you card. Don't put your name or address on it and don't sign it. Inside, write, "Just thought you should know you're appreciated". Disguise your handwriting and never tell.

10. When no one is watching, put a coin on the street. Then watch out of the way to see who finds it and how they react. If you're feeling generous, make it a fiver.

11. Get on a bus or underground train going in any direction. Take a pack of cards with you. Take out a card at random. The value of this card is the number of stops you'll go before you get out and walk around for an hour (picture cards = 10).

12. Go into a toy shop and buy a simple toy you had as a child (for example, a yo-yo or some modelling clay). Take an hour at the weekend to play with it (secretly, if you fear ridicule).

13. Take a walk and imagine you are your favourite character from a book or film. How would they see this world?

What would this person's feelings be about the things they encounter? If you're feeling brave, have a chat with someone while staying in character (in other words, talk like your character, too).

14. Go into a restaurant that features food you seldom eat. Let the waiter or waitress order for you.

15. Buy a session in a flotation tank. If that's not possible, sit in a bathtub full of water that's at body temperature, turn off the lights, use earplugs, sit back and let your mind drift.

16. Watch a TV station that broadcasts in a language you don't understand. Make up your own translations of the dialogue. Start with the assumption it's a science fiction show, then that it's a comedy, then that it's a soap opera.

17. Lie down on the floor of your wardrobe and look up.

18. Pick the most recent big thing that's happened to you. Pretend it was sent to you as a valuable lesson. What is there to learn from the experience?

19. Pretend you're Einstein, on his first day on the job you usually do. What would he ask? What would he do?

20. Think about a good friend from your childhood, someone you're no longer in touch with. Take five minutes to create a biography of what you think has happened to them since.

21 Write a crazy personals ad. If you feel like it, actually put it in a magazine and see what kind of answers you get. Answer all the letters you get (but you don't necessarily have to give them your name and address ...).

22. Get a comic strip, cover up all the dialogue with Tippex and write new dialogue.

23. For a day, listen at least three times as much as you talk. Notice any difference in how people react to you.

24. For a day, carry a coin in your pocket. Make all minor decisions based on flipping the coin.

25. At the beginning of the day, write your own horoscope. During the course of the day, see how much of it you can make come true.

26. In a bookshop read the last 10 pages of a thriller or crime novel. Try to figure out what happened before.

27. Get a postcard. Paste a photo of your office or work area over the front. Write on the back that you're enjoying yourself (you are, aren't you?) and tell a little about what you're doing. Post it to a friend or relative.

28. The next time you ask someone how they are and they say a perfunctory "Fine", say, "That's great ... what's the best thing that's happening at the moment?"

29. Make yourself an impressive-looking diploma or award for something you're proud to have done. Frame it and hang it on your wall. Feel free to use the Wolff Institute

OK, Peter, maybe not
quite that much
playfulness...

of Advanced Focus and Creativity as the rewarding insti-
tution – I believe in you.

30. Make your own Ten Commandments. Unlike the original,
    focus on what thou shalt rather than what thou shalt not
    do.

These 30 creative acts are only a start, of course. Why not
begin each month by coming up with 30 of your own ideas?
And if you have friends who are forgetting to spend time on
fun and creative stimulation, write one of the ideas above, or
one of your own, on a postcard and send it to them and invite
them to send their ideas back for you.

With a sense of playfulness, a sense of balance, and enough
time for rest and exercise, you will find it easy to maintain
your ability to focus on and achieve your most cherished
goals. The final chapter of this book provides you with a
roadmap you can follow each time you set a new goal for
yourself.

Website chapter bonus

At www.focusquick.com you'll find an interview with life
coach Carol Thompson on creating a balanced life.

16

How to put it all together to reach all your goals

If you did all the exercises in this book as you read it, you'll already have moved a long way toward your goals. However, many people prefer to read a book like this through once and then go back and do the work. For your convenience, in this chapter you'll find a reminder of all the key points and major steps in one place so that you can easily apply the Focus process to every goal and project you have from now on.

Define what you want from applying the Focus process

What is the biggest change you'd like to make in your life by applying the techniques that make up the Focus process?

STEP 1: Analyse your 80/20 time

- In many aspects of life, it's only 20% of what you do that gives you 80% of your good results.

- Focusing your attention on what is positive is the fastest route to success.

- By identifying the three activities that you do that add most value, and seeing how much (or little) time you spend on them currently, you can see how much room for improvement there is for allocating your time for better results.

- It's human nature to stick with things that aren't paying off in value or enjoyment, but by overcoming old habits you will move ahead of the pack in achievement and enjoyment.

In the context of work, what is giving you the greatest value now?

_____

_____

_____

In your personal life, what is giving you the greatest value now?

_____

_____

_____

In your work life, what are three activities you aren't doing but that could contribute great value?

_____

_____

_____

In your personal life, what are three activities you aren't doing but that could contribute great value?

_____

_____

_____

In your work life, what is one old habit that represents the less valuable 80% of your time use? (This will be a good candidate for elimination.)

_____

In your personal life, what is one old habit that represents the less valuable 80% of your time use? (Another good candidate for elimination.)

_____

STEP 2: Set Your first goal

- Goals should be positive, specific and measurable.

- They should also be attainable and realistic – but you are the one to decide what is attainable and realistic, and it will be based on how much effort you are prepared to make. Big goals are motivational.

- The usual emphasis on setting hard deadlines for goals dooms many of them to failure because almost every goal involves elements whose duration you can't predict. Use hard deadlines only for tasks within your control.

- When you commit to changing your strategies until you find the ones that work, you eliminate failure as an option. The only way to fail is to stop.

- You can break down big goals into smaller goals and decide what tasks you need to do to achieve them. Goal maps are a good way to diagram this.

● Picturing your quest to reach your goals as a hero's journey can help keep you motivated.

Write down one goal that is big enough to be exciting and motivational and to which you are ready to commit your time and energy. Make sure to express it in positive terms (what you want, not what you don't want).

_____

_____

_____

How will you know when you have achieved the goal? How will you measure this?

_____

What are three sub-goals you will need to reach on the way to the goal? You can list them below and then use software or just pens and a large sheet of paper to expand this with as many related tasks as you can think of in a goal map for each sub-goal. If necessary, use the visualisation and the hero's journey sentence completion exercise in Chapter 2 to come up with further ideas about the steps on the road to your goal (repeating these two may give you fresh ideas each time you do it).

_____

_____

_____

If you had to make up a superhero's name for yourself as you embark on this goal, what would it be?

_____

The creation of goal maps is the most important part of the planning process, so don't expect to do it all in one session.

You can continue to expand and refine them as you work through the rest of this chapter.

STEP 3: Examine and change your time patterns

- We all have some patterns of behaviour that we repeat even though they don't give us the results we want.

- It's important to identify which patterns are holding you back.

- Even patterns that have mostly negative results give us some kind of pay-off – usually it's protection from the possibility of rejection or failure.

- Once you identify the pay-offs you're getting from your negative patterns, you can figure out how to get the same pay-offs from positive patterns. This is the key to making lasting changes in any part of your life.

As you look back on your life so far, what patterns do you detect that may have limited your success? These might relate to beliefs, habits, behaviour, relationships, or any other facets of your life. Unless you're a combination of Mother Teresa, Bill Gates, and Nelson Mandela, you should be able to find some. In Chapter 3, we looked mainly at patterns of time use, but now that you're putting it all together, think bigger.

_____

_____

_____

What pay-offs do you think you received from each of these?

_____

_____

_____

For each of the pay-offs, come up with one way you could get the same or a similar pay-off without the drawbacks of the patterns you've had in the past. This may take some time and deep thought.

_____

_____

_____

For each of the new strategies or behaviours you've identified, write down how they are likely to help you achieve the goal you've set for yourself.

_____

_____

_____

STEP 4: Overcome the most common obstacles

- To make more time for your goals you have to find ways to reduce the time you're spending on less important activities.

- You can save 10% of your time by finding tasks or activities that can be eliminated.

- You can save another 10% by delegating tasks. You can hire students or use online virtual assistants and project freelancers.

- The reason people don't do some crucial tasks is simply that they are less enjoyable to do than others, but you can find ways to make them more appealing.

- One way to make tasks less daunting is to chunk them down into very small steps. Another is to create the conditions that allow you to get into a "flow" state.

- You can also take advantage of small chunks of time you carve out of your schedule.

What are one to three ways you spend time now that you can eliminate or reduce in order to have more time to dedicate to reaching your goal?

_____

_____

_____

What are one to three ways you spend time now that you can delegate in order to have more time to dedicate to reaching your goals? Also indicate to whom you will delegate them.

_____

_____

_____

What are three tasks that you will continue to have to do that you find in some way unpleasant or tedious?

_____

_____

_____

For each one, list one way you can make it more enjoyable, or at least more bearable. Possible strategies include chunking it down, linking it with an activity you do enjoy, and creating a flow state.

_____

_____

_____

STEP 5: Leverage what already works

- Before you can put your strengths to their best use, you must know what they are.

- Always focus on using your strengths rather than trying to improve your weaknesses.

- With any necessary tasks that you generally don't do well, notice what's different about the times you *do* perform them well. Use what you learn from the exceptions to make them the rule.

- Notice when things are going well and consider what's responsible, so that you can use the same methods in other situations.

- When you are functioning especially well, link that activity to a sound or a pleasant smell. When you need to function that way again use the sound or odour to prompt the right mood.

- Be aware of when and where you have your best ideas. Don't overlook the contribution of daydreams and night dreams.

❝Always focus on using your strengths❞

In your work life, what are your three greatest strengths?

_____

_____

_____

In your personal life, what are your three greatest strengths?

_____

_____

_____

What new ideas do you now have for how you can leverage these strengths in order to achieve your goal?

_____

_____

_____

Select one issue on which you'd like to get greater clarity. Take 15 minutes to daydream about it – not trying to force a solution, just letting your mind wander around it – and then note any insights that come up.

_____

_____

_____

For the same issue or a different one, experiment tonight with posing a question about it just before you go to sleep. In the morning, remember any dreams, or even dream fragments, you experienced and describe how they might shed some new light on the situation.

_____

_____

_____

STEP 6: Finally overcome procrastination

- Leaving things to the last minute is a problem only if it causes you to miss deadlines, do lower quality work, or feel stressed.

- Procrastination generally comes from the fact that the alternative is appealing right now, whereas the rewards of doing what you're avoiding are in the future.

- You can make future benefits stronger by vividly imagining them using all your senses.

- You can create an "anchor" that will help you get in the right state of mind to overcome procrastination.

- If you're unsure of the reasons behind your procrastination, you can find out more by using the sentence completion technique.

- The "chunking down" strategy makes it easy to get started and to continue to get your work done.

- Your personality type and the Alter Ego strategy can help you accomplish everything on your to do list.

Is procrastination a problem for you? If not, skip this section. Otherwise, write down three situations or tasks you often procrastinate about.

_____

_____

_____

For each of these situations, write down a compelling vision of the outcome you are going for. For instance, if you always put off preparing tax returns (and you can't delegate it), jot down in as specific terms as possible how great it will feel to be finished with this task.

_____

_____

_____

_____

_____

_____

PUTTING IT ALL TOGETHER

If you haven't done so already, create an anchor for a state of mind/body in which you feel energetic and ready to tackle even previously unpleasant chores. If you need to review the process, go back to Chapter 6. If you need to strengthen the anchor, just repeat the exercise a few times.

Describe one task you've been putting off that you will do today (or at least start on), as well as the strategy you will apply for overcoming your impulse to procrastinate in this situation. If you need more help, go back and do (or repeat) the sentence completion technique and the personality analysis featured in Chapter 6.

_____

_____

_____

STEP 7: Use the Alter Ego strategy

- You have many different personalities that emerge based on the situation in which you find yourself.

- You can choose which personality to put in charge at any given time, to make sure that it's the one best equipped to handle the task you want to achieve.

- It's helpful to give these Alter Egos names that help you capture the essence of their personality. Examples include Attila, Miss Moneypenny, The Consultant and The Arch-Villain.

What names can you give three or more Alter Egos that are part of your larger personality? (You already came up with one for your superhero character.)

_____

_____

_____

Refer to your goal map and choose three of the next steps you will take. For each one identify which of your Alter Egos should be in charge of that task.

_____

_____

_____

STEP 8: Train other people to support and help you

- You can train the people around you to be supportive.
- The number one thing people crave is recognition.
- Ways you can give people recognition include listening, increasing eye contact, using their names, giving compliments and asking for their opinions.
- Always reward behaviour that you'd like to see repeated.

Is there anyone in your life from whom you would like to have more support? If so, list their names here.

_____

_____

_____

What strategies will you use to get these people to be more supportive?

_____

_____

_____

What ways will you use to give more recognition to the people who do support you or whose efforts are important to you? Name the person and the methods you will employ.

_____

_____

_____

_____

STEP 9: Focus your language

- Most conversations are merely intersecting monologues. You can transform them into true communication by actually listening.

- You can establish rapport with someone else by finding or creating things in common and by subtly matching the language of their representational system (visual, auditory, kinaesthetic).

- To persuade someone, start where they are and then lead them in your direction, in a process known as pacing and leading.

- Another powerful communication tool is reframing, which means changing the context or meaning of something by putting it into a different perspective.

- You can deal with opposition by exploring it by asking at least three questions about the reasons behind it.

- When you can't agree it can help to take a step back and find the last thing you did agree about and generate alternatives from that.

- Some people are in the habit of automatically opposing every suggestion; you can handle this polarity response by giving them alternatives to choose from, or by suggesting the opposite of what you really want.

Choose three people from your personal or work life and practise your listening skills with them over the next few days. Jot down their names and what you perceive to be their primary representational system (visual, auditory, kinaesthetic) based on their language.

_____

_____

_____

In the next couple of days find at least one opportunity to pace and lead to bring someone to a more constructive or positive point of agreement. Note your observations and anything you learned in the process.

_____

_____

_____

Find at least one opportunity to use reframing, either with yourself or another person. Again, note your observations.

_____

_____

_____

The next time you encounter opposition or disagreement, try out whichever technique seems most likely to be effective: the three questions approach, stepping back to the last point of agreement, or turning polarity back on the other person. Note your observations.

STEP 10: Create information focus

- We are being swamped with more information than ever before and one result is noise pollution that can cause stress and overload.

- It is easier to filter out the irrelevant information when you have a purpose in mind.

- Some information, especially on the internet, comes from biased or unqualified sources who may have a hidden agenda. That makes it important to double-check your sources.

- If you are aware of your learning style you can select information that is easier to process and absorb.

- True peak performers don't subscribe to the idea of being connected 24/7. It's important to have quiet time for thought and reflection.

Is information overload a problem for you? If not, skip this section. Otherwise, write down three types of information overload that cause you stress.

For each of these issues, select at least one strategy from Chapter 10 to combat the overload (among others, these include reducing noise, setting out a clear purpose before reading anything, and using your answering machine).

_____

_____

_____

What will you do in order to have some time every day when you are not at anybody else's beck and call and have time for reflection?

_____

_____

_____

STEP 11: Climb the paperwork mountain

- A messy desk or office is a problem only if it's a problem.

- Once you know whether you are more of a right-brain or left-brain person, you can choose your organisational tools accordingly.

- Handling each piece of paper only once is ideal but not always realistic.

- A filing system that allows you to see the material will be more satisfying and effective for right-brain people.

- You can use the power of lists to streamline almost any repetitive task.

- Your daily to-do list should contain only the tasks you are committed to achieving that day. The rest belong on a master list.

- Using a combination of daily and monthly folders makes it easy to schedule future tasks.

Are you unhappy with your current systems of dealing with paperwork? If not, skip this section. Otherwise, write down what you believe are the three things that are creating the biggest problems.

_____

_____

_____

If your filing system isn't working, set up the system described in Chapter 11, using letter and number combinations and a master list. How might this help solve the problems you have just listed?

_____

If your task organisation and timing are a problem, set up the 31 days/12 months folder system described in Chapter 11. How might this help solve any of the problems you have just listed?

_____

If your daily to do list isn't working, adopt the format described in Chapter 11, limiting the list to only the tasks you genuinely are committed to achieving that day. How might this help solve any of the problems you have just listed?

_____

If you or the people you work with are frequently handling the same challenges, set up a system of lists so that the problems or tasks can be handled quickly and in a manner that has been shown to work. How might this help solve any of the problems you have just listed?

_____

If any of the problems you listed cannot be handled with these techniques, go back over the additional suggestions mentioned in Chapter 11.

STEP 12: Tame the email monster

- Read email only at set points during the day.
- Be ruthless about deleting – use the Alter Ego strategy.
- Guide others as to the kinds of emails you want and don't want.
- Whenever possible, delegate.
- Set up an email filing system that mirrors your real filing system.
- Use the subject line of your emails to give as much information as possible.
- Never use emails for sensitive messages about others or about yourself.
- In your emails, provide context, be brief, and be specific about what actions you expect from the recipient.

Is handling email a problem for you? If not, skip this section (and congratulations!). Otherwise, describe your main email challenges (which could include feeling compelled to check it too frequently, taking too much time to answer it, etc.).

_____

_____

_____

For each of these, list at least one strategy from the summary points above or from Chapter 12 that you will employ to solve the problem.

_____

_____

_____

Choose at least one of these strategies and implement it immediately. Do it for several days and note the impact here.

_____

_____

_____

After a few days, add another strategy and implement it and again note the results.

_____

_____

_____

You can continue the process until you have email totally under control. This is one task which requires constant vigilance!

STEP 13: Master meetings and networking

- The easiest way to deal with boring meetings is to skip them or to attend only the portion that really concerns you.

- Meetings should have a clear purpose and agenda, time limits, and rules for conduct. The latter should specify no phone calls or texting.

- In brainstorming meetings, follow the four guidelines in

order to maintain the flow of ideas: quantity, no judgement, write everything down, and build on previous ideas.

- Keep meetings as low-tech as possible (avoid PowerPoint).
- Traditional networking meetings tend to be a waste of time and excruciating for a lot of the people attending them. Use the Alter Ego strategy when you choose to attend the 20% of such meetings that are most useful.
- You can network virtually and use websites, blogs, podcasts, and articles to share your knowledge and get people to come to you.

Meetings

Are meetings a problem for you? If not, skip the first part of this section and proceed to the networking section. Otherwise, write down the three biggest meetings issues that cause you problems. These might include too many meetings, meetings that are too long, disorganised meetings, etc.

_____

_____

_____

Are there any meetings that you now attend that you could miss, or at least attend only relevant portions of them?

_____

_____

_____

For meetings you do have to attend, what changes would
have the greatest effect in making them more efficient? This
could include setting clearer agendas, enforcing rules such as
no texting, and eliminating technology.

_____

_____

_____

Networking

Is networking something you enjoy? If so, skip the rest of this
section. If not, list the three things you dislike the most about
networking.

_____

_____

_____

Which of the techniques recommended in Chapter 13 could
you apply in order to make networking less painful and more
productive? Name one Alter Ego you could use to help.

_____

_____

_____

How could you replace traditional networking with internet
techniques that will motivate people to come to you? If
appropriate, go back to your goal map and see where these
techniques will fit in.

_____

_____

_____

STEP 14: Deal with deadlines and multiple projects

- The best way to figure out the steps to your goal is working backward from the result you want.

- You can use your previous history to improve the accuracy of your estimates of how long each task or step will take.

- Apply the three D's (Delete, Delegate, Do) at each step of the process.

- Inspect, don't expect.

- It's important to be flexible about how you reach your goals.

- When problems arise, isolate them and immediately set about solving them.

- There is a constructive way to panic if a project goes off the rails.

- When you handle multiple projects, look for synergies between them and try to time them so they don't share the same deadline dates.

At this point you will probably have already created your goal maps (if not, do so now). You can further refine these maps now, starting with an assessment of how accurate you tend to be at estimating how long things will take. If you typically underestimate, go back now and add the necessary leeway to make sure it will not happen this time.

Also re-inspect each step on the map to double-check that you have not missed any opportunities to delete or delegate.

Next, add inspection points on the map, for the times when you will check to make sure that the people who are contributing to your goal are achieving their tasks at the agreed-upon pace.

If you are pursuing more than one goal, look at all the goal maps and find any possible synergies that will save time and effort.

Finally, if you encounter unexpected obstacles, be prepared to isolate them and solve them immediately and, as a last resort, panic constructively.

STEP 15: Maintaining your new found focus

- To ensure balance, have goals for each of the important aspects of your life.
- Cutting back on sleep or exercise are false economies. Sufficient sleep and exercise will help you to work and play at full effectiveness.
- Schedule at least small chunks of time for relaxation to overcome the effects of stress.
- Playfulness is a crucial component of creativity. Find some play time every day.

Do you have goals for each major part of your life? If not, generate some that will help you ensure that you will give adequate time to every major part of your life.

Health and fitness goal: _____

Family relationships goal: _____

Friends relationships goal: _____

Spiritual goal: _____

Community goal: _____

Any other area of life important to you:_____

You can go through the Focus process for each of these goals.

What is one way you get healthful exercise at least three times a week? If none currently, what will you schedule?

_____

What is one playful element in your life that gives you pleasure and allows you to relax? If none currently, what will you schedule?

_____

This is not the end, it is the start . . .

This is the start of your journey of achieving goal after goal with an ease that others will admire. Come back to this book whenever you are uncertain of what to do next, and also check the www.focusquick.com website frequently because we will be updating it and adding new resources. The website will also allow you to email me directly. If you have any questions, don't hesitate to contact me and I will try to help. I'd also love to hear of the successes you have by following the Focus strategies – nothing would make me happier than to join you in celebrating your achievements!

HAPPY AT WORK

Ten Steps to Ultimate Job Satisfaction

Sophie Rowan
9780273714231
£9.99

Discover happiness at work with this life changing guide.

Making even the smallest change to your work life makes a big difference to your happiness

Learn how to:

Manage Yourself

Manage Others

Manage Your World of Work

BUILD YOUR FOUNDATIONS OF HAPPINESS